W9-DCC-649

If At First...

If At

Adela

First...

Holzer

Stein and Day/*Publishers*/New York

First published in 1977

Printed in the United States of America
Stein and Day/*Publishers*/Scarborough House,
Briarcliff Manor, N.Y. 10510

Library of Congress Cataloging in Publication Data

Holzer, Adela.
If at first . . .

1. Holzer, Adela. 2. Theatrical producers and directors—United States—Biography. I. Title.
PN2287.H62A34 792'.0232'0924 [B] 77-9610
ISBN 0-8128-2145-9

To my beloved son, Carlos

Without your undying support none of this could have been possible.
Through our most difficult and trying times, it was your unbounding love and understanding that proved to be the most important reason I needed to continue in the face of all adversity.

To thank you would be insufficient, to love you is the most I can give.

Preface

I was an immigrant to the United States, a stranger painfully learning American customs, so I was scarcely aware of the campaign for equality being waged by American women. I don't mean to sound smug, but I was too busy finding myself as a person, earning a living for my children and myself.

Thanks to my ignorance, it took me a long time to realize I was regarded as something of a celebrity. I knew I had achieved success in the world, of course, but I didn't think it mattered to anyone but me.

Friends have persuaded me that my story is worth telling, in the hope that I can help other women who are struggling against odds that seem to overwhelm them. So here I am, revealing my weaknesses as well as my strengths, my good fortune and my bad.

A word in private to the women who are still struggling: What I have done, you can do.

If At First...

One

I was born with the proverbial silver spoon in my mouth, but it took me a long time to realize that silver tarnishes.

I am a native of Madrid and was born in 1934 at a time when Spain was edging ever closer to the precipice of civil war. My father was an attorney by profession, but he had become an industrialist, which is a polite way of saying he bought companies, managed companies and sold companies. My mother was a Spanish lady, which is a less than polite way of saying she had been prepared only for the life of a social ornament. She knew nothing about the harsh realities of the world.

My parents' home was large and very dark, filled with heavy furniture and located in one of Madrid's most fashionable residential districts. It took me many years to sense that the lavish decor was depressing. It stifled me, and still does.

The first thing in my life that I can remember was an incident that took place when I was a fragile three-year-old girl with short, red hair and bangs. For some unknown reason I was wearing a white dress, trimmed with lace, the kind usually reserved for mass on Sunday mornings.

I was unattended, which was unusual, allowed to wander where I pleased, and I found myself in one of the many living rooms. There was a full length mirror set in a wall, and being a vain little creature, I paused to admire myself. In the reflection of the mirror I noticed a handsome, beautifully dressed man come into the room. As I turned he saw me and snapped my photograph with a camera he was carrying.

That man was my father, and I was pleased because I had caught his attention, something that didn't happen often. However, my joy was fleeting; my father, followed by the secretary who was always at his heels, disappeared again.

It was clear to me that nobody else thought I was pretty. I turned back to the mirror. A number of other people bustled through the room, but I paid no more attention to them than they did to me. *I* thought I was cute, even if no one else cared.

My new German governess found me in front of the mirror, just as I forgot myself long enough to stare at a lovely, lace-trimmed crib that someone was carrying. "That's too big for my dolls," I told her, but she didn't answer.

After she hauled me off to my playroom she told me some men from Paris had left a cradle at our house with a baby in it. The Spanish equivalent of the stork story.

I had seen the crib but not the baby, so I must have looked skeptical.

"You don't believe you have a sister?" she demanded in the sarcastic tone I came to hate.

The governess didn't understand. I had been an only child who had never known a playmate, and I didn't want a stranger intruding into my private world.

Several days passed before I was taken to see my sister, and I was horrified when I saw an infant rather than someone of my own age. No one had bothered to prepare me for her arrival, and I wanted nothing to do with her. The gulf that separated my sister and me existed from the time of her birth.

As far back as I can remember I was withdrawn, and as the years passed I became even more introverted. I had no alternative. My favorite pastime was being allowed to spend a few moments in one of the drawing rooms—salons that were labeled yellow, blue, green or white, depending on the color of the velvet or damask drapes and the sofa that invariably matched them.

The walls of these rooms were filled with magnificent paintings. As I later learned, my father collected art works of the fifteenth through the eighteenth centuries. All I knew at the time was that these paintings fired my imagination, keeping my mind busy for days. There were so many of them that I couldn't absorb all of them during the brief time I was allowed to stay in a drawing room, so I taught myself a special memory technique. When I was called into a room I concentrated my complete attention on a single wall, transferring the paintings to my memory while paying little attention to what my parents might be saying to me.

Certainly I learned early in life that my parents merely went through the motions of receiving me for a few minutes each day. Not until I became an adult did it dawn on me that my father, who had wanted a son, felt disappointed whenever he saw me, or that my mother, who was the victim of her own childhood environment, cared only about herself.

My life was filled with prohibitions. I wasn't allowed to draw pictures near my sister because I might infect her with germs; I don't know how long I believed she was germ-free, and that I was laden with them. I was not allowed to touch antiques, precious bric-a-brac or rare books, and when I disobeyed—which I did frequently—the governess slapped me. I still cringe at the sound of a slap, and it isn't accidental that my own home is filled with bric-a-brac that members of my family are free to handle.

Worst of all, I was not allowed to play with my marvelous collection of dolls. They sat dressed in their lovely, colorful gowns in rows on shelves, and I could only stare at them. As a special treat after mass on Sundays, if I had behaved during the week, I was permitted to play with my dolls for a short time. However, I delighted in caressing the beautiful dolls when nobody was around.

Soon after my sister was born, my governess began to tutor me. My days were filled with lessons from early morning until bedtime. I learned to read and write. I studied arithmetic. I was taught German, English, French. And I must admit, I'm grateful now that I became adept in languages. In the afternoons I was taught ladylike pursuits, and learned to play the piano and to sew. From a very early age I was required to knit my own socks and to darn them when they developed holes.

Thanks to the intercession of my darling, tender grandfather, I was allowed to dine with the adults once each year, on Christmas Eve. I took no active part in the conversation, which was confined to politics and finance, but occasionally my father quizzed me to make sure I paid attention.

I have never forgotten the coral music room, and I still remember the guilded Louis XV sofa and armchairs, the Gobelin tapestry with a scene from *Don Quixote,* the fragile eighteenth century piano made in England. There were French chests covered with inlaid marble, a splendid antique mirror and a magnificent La Granja chandelier.

In my innocence I believed everyone lived as we did, and I actually thought the coral room was cozy. My favorites were porcelain figurines scattered around the room. My grandfather explained them to me in great detail, even telling me where they had been made and by whom.

Everything in our house, including the table service, had been made prior to the nineteenth century, because my father believed that workmanship became shoddy by the 1800s. As a direct result, my sister and I found it very difficult to sit on the chairs, which were either too fragile or too high for us. But we learned sooner than most to appreciate antiques and works of art.

To the eternal credit of my parents, the monetary worth of their belongings was never mentioned, and instead they emphasized the love that had gone into the making of each piece. I was nineteen before I realized that our antiques were priceless. A newspaper reporter managed to infiltrate my sister's debutante party, and I was astonished when I read the next day that our belongings were so valuable.

My father, who hated publicity, paced up and down the room roaring and, after he calmed down, he lectured me. Publicity was evil, and I should never allow anyone to take my picture. It seems that when he had been a lawyer he heard of an attempt to blackmail a wealthy girl by superimposing a picture of a naked body over her photo. My father had retreated into privacy to protect himself and his family, and my sister and I were expected to follow his example.

Soon after I became conscious of it, our splendid style of living was interrupted for three years by the Spanish civil war, one of the most vicious struggles in the tortured history of this century. My father, who disliked politicians of all persuasions and thought of himself exclusively as a businessman, discreetly went off to Portugal until he could see which way the winds of war were blowing. My mother, who didn't know right from left—the forces of Franco from the Loyalists—stayed behind with two small daughters.

Madrid was held by the Loyalists, and soon everyone in the city wore something red as a symbol. Our servants became informants, militiamen visited our house regularly, sometimes stealing works of art, and even as a small child I was aware of the atmosphere of fear. When the shooting started, my governess left Spain for Germany without delay, so there was at least one streak of sunshine in the gloom.

Violent atrocities were committed by both sides during the civil war. I was present at one that I cannot forget. My grandfather was a prominent liberal, a member of the Republican party and the president of a number of charitable organizations, so the family assumed he was safe in Madrid.

One day, when my mother, my baby sister and I were visiting him, I nicked my finger while cutting a hard piece of chocolate, and my grandfather picked me up to comfort me. While I was sitting on his lap a squad of militiamen arrived.

The instant he identified himself, a soldier put a bullet through his neck, barely missing me. As I tumbled to the floor the other members of the squad fired shot after shot into him.

Not realizing what I was doing, I mixed my grandfather's blood with that of my cut finger, smearing my white dress, as I had seen gypsies do at their weddings. With sudden terror I realized my grandfather was dead and I ran from the room screaming.

For weeks I was numb, and my mother could scarcely function.

Much later my uncle was told the supposed reason for the senseless murder. Since my grandfather was one of Spain's leading art authorities, the Loyalist government had asked him to appraise some of the great paintings in the Prado Museum. They intended to send these works to Moscow as payment for arms and munitions they were buying from Russia. My grandfather knew of the plan, and the Loyalists, afraid of the public reaction if the word leaked out that they were selling the nation's treasures, had him murdered.

His house was ransacked, and all his precious artworks vanished. A few years ago I was stunned when I saw one of them on exhibition at the Cloisters in New York City. To this day I have no idea how it fell into the hands of the dealers who sold it.

I try to forget the civil war, but there are some scenes I cannot put permanently from my mind. One of the worst happened one night, when I heard noises on our street. I looked out the window and saw people being burned alive as human torches. Later I was told they were priests and nuns.

In 1938, during one of the visits of the militia to our house, they took my mother with them to open her bank vault. She did not return, and I was frantic.

I was barely old enough to call my uncle's house on the telephone, but there was no answer, and small wonder. Most of our relatives had gone into hiding. All of our servants except two had deserted us, and I was afraid that they would turn my sister and me over to the authorities who were sending orphans off to Russia.

In my desperation I had just enough sense to find my sister's wet nurse, who was loyal to the family, and she gave us sanctuary in her tiny, cramped quarters. For the first time I knew the meaning of real love and began to learn, too, how most people in Spain lived. My sister and I slept in one bed, and often we were hungry.

In spite of the dangers, the nurse was determined to find out what had become of my mother, and day after day she searched the city making inquiries. Sometimes, when mobs were looting and it wasn't safe to leave my sister and me behind, she took us with her. We became accustomed to the daily bombings of Madrid by Franco's air force. One day we saw a Russian plane spray machine-gun bullets at people standing in a breadline. The plane had flimsy Fascist over-markings, but it was shot down, and these markings fell off, revealing its real identity. Much later I was told the purpose of the deception had been to create even greater hatred toward the Franco forces.

At last the nurse located my mother, and the next day she took my sister and me to the *cheka,* the Russian name that the people had given to the prison. My mother was crowded into a cell no more than forty feet long and thirty feet wide; at least one hundred fifty others were there too, and only a few could even lie down at one time.

It took me quite a while to recognize my mother. In three months she had lost more than forty pounds, her hair had turned white and her body was racked by a deep cough. The worst shock was that she didn't seem to know me, and I had to tug at her sleeve through the bars before she even acknowledged my presence. Several times she reached out and touched my sister, but her face was drained of all expression.

Finally she spoke, and began to weep; as she clutched the bars I saw that her fingers were swollen. "Bring me a blanket and take me out of here," she said. It was the first time I had ever seen her weep.

Not until I was older did I learn that no charges had been brought against her, and she had received no prison sentence. The Loyalists had not questioned her, and as she herself knew literally nothing about politics she had no idea why she was being held. When she asked her jailers for information they just shrugged.

I didn't see my mother in prison again, but I thought about her constantly, exaggerating all her good qualities in my mind, the way one does a close relative who has died. In short, I idolized her until she left the jail.

A few months before the war ended a group representing some foreign humanitarian organization—it may have been the International Red Cross—paid a visit to the women's prison and filed a report saying the cells were so crowded that inmates were forced to live under subhuman conditions. The Loyalists disliked the publicity, so a number of prisoners were released. My mother was one of them, and she was set free as casually as she had been taken into custody. There were no hearings of any kind; the jailers simply scratched my mother's name off the list and told her to go home. To this day she doesn't know why she was arrested and held.

My mother went home, then traced my sister and me, and we rejoined her. After nineteen months of imprisonment she had no understanding of the outside world. I found it very difficult to persuade her that she had to get up at four in the morning to join the breadline with the rest of us, and that if she wasn't there in person we would be given one portion less.

I wasn't yet six years old, but the war had toughened me, and when I realized that my mother couldn't take responsibility, I went from the breadline to another where oranges were given out. For months we lived on bread and orange peels that we fried in questionable grease. Luckily I had a child's imagination and pretended they were potatoes.

So many buildings had been gutted by bombs that housing was at a premium, and we found about twenty-five people, all of them refugees, taking shelter in our house. We felt like intruders in our own home.

I was fortunate, however, because one of the refugees was a primary-school teacher who took a liking to me and taught me elementary geography and history. I worked hard, not only because I was eager to learn just for the sake of acquiring knowledge, but because I wanted to be able to impress my father when I saw him again.

I could scarcely remember him, but I clung to my few memories, expanding them in my mind and convincing myself that we had been very close. This fantasy was doubly important to me because my relations with my mother were so unsatisfactory.

During the year and a half of her imprisonment I had chosen to forget her indifference to me. Now that we were together again, I could no longer ignore the fact that she cared very little for me. It was obvious to everyone that she preferred my sister, paid scant attention to me and was relieved when I wasn't in her company.

In all fairness to her, she was suffering from tuberculosis and a kidney infection. Madrid was besieged by Franco's armies, with the result that food became increasingly scarce and medicines were unavailable.

Thanks to friends who went to the Red Cross, we were given permission to go to France. But to obtain exit permits, we were instructed to pretend that my father had been killed. At the crucial moment in the visa interview my mother started to blunder, so I covered quickly with a convincing story about my father's death. After we were given the permits I shouted at my mother and called her stupid—something unheard of in our kind of society, and she never forgave me.

Soon after we reached France we heard from my father. Working from his base in Portugal, he had been waiting to see the outcome of the war. When it became apparent that Franco would win, he moved to Franco's zone. He owned various properties in the Basque provinces, which are located in the north of Spain, and was granted permission to go there. He quickly made the arrangements for us to cross the border from France and join him.

I shall never forget our reunion. My father looked much older, so I didn't know him and neither did my sister, of course, as she had been a baby when he had fled to Portugal. He didn't recognize *any* of us. My mother's appearance had changed drastically, my sister was now a little girl rather than an infant, and I had grown tall and was very thin. When my mother called out to him he stared at us for a moment, and then wept as he embraced us. It is the only time in my life I have ever seen my father shed tears.

My joy over our reunion was short-lived. My father decided we would stay in the north until we could return to Madrid, and I was sent to a Basque school for girls.

The Basques do not consider themselves Spaniards. They are a rough, fiercely independent people with their own language, customs and traditions, and many of them have little use for Castilians. We, of course, were Castilians.

I was the outsider at school, unable to make friends, sometimes shunned and sometimes teased by girls with whom I had almost nothing in common. I was an alien in a strange world, old beyond my years because of my wartime experiences in Madrid, and I was miserable.

I was also a very lonely child. My father, making up for lost time, spent all his time and energies restoring his businesses. My mother devoted herself to her health and made a determined effort to forget the war. Unfortunately for me, this prevented her from giving me the attention I would have liked.

My father got in touch with my hated German governess, and—much to my dismay—she returned. She was a very strict disciplinarian, a sadist, and having become a mystic since we had last seen her, she made a determined effort to convert everyone else. I was her prime target.

Thanks to the resilience I had acquired during the war and the innate toughness of spirit I inherited from my father, I was able to fight her. Our battle was unending, and I was convinced it would be the end of me if I gave in. On the slightest pretext she slapped, pinched or spanked me, and I gave her ample reason. The nastier she became the more I turned into a little monster, defying her to break my spirit.

Fräulein Marie, the governess, truly hated me, and because my mother paid no attention to me the harridan could treat me as she pleased. Severe daily beatings were normal, and often her punishments were cruel. On one occasion, because I had cried during a visit to the dentist, she shut me in a small, dark closet for three days and nights, giving me only bread and water. But the more vicious she became, the harder I fought.

Looking back on my early childhood, I realize now that whatever strength of character I may have acquired is due, at least in part, to my private war with my governess. That war lasted for two years, by which time we had returned to our house in Madrid. The governess finally surrendered, and when she complained to my parents that she couldn't handle me, it was decided that I would attend a convent school.

The nuns were strict, as those who have attended parochial schools anywhere well know, but to me my new school was heaven on earth. I loved every minute of my life there, and carried my enthusiasm to extremes. When I caught various childhood diseases like chicken pox and measles I concealed my illness as long as I could, not wanting to miss even one day of school. Naturally, I infected my whole class each time, and I don't think the good sisters quite appreciated my zeal.

In the meantime, World War II had begun. To Spaniards it meant slower rebuilding of a country nearly destroyed by a cruel civil war and continuing famine. To me it seemed that Europe had become a wasteland full of the darkest horrors. Cities were decimated and in my childish imagination the absurdity of the war became clear after seeing Spain being nearly annihilated. Why didn't the rest of Europe learn instead of repeating the same mistake?

I didn't understand that my early childhood was unusual. I had taken our wealth for granted. I learned during the war that physical possessions are an illusion. I learned there is nothing more important than food when one is hungry. Above all, I learned the need for spiritual nourishment. My father's preoccupation with his work and my mother's absorption with herself taught me that human beings must have love if they are to be fulfilled.

All I knew as a child, however, was that I had to work harder than anyone else and really make something of myself if I wanted attention. I didn't realize it, but I was already preparing myself for a life that some people call extraordinary.

Two

Work! By the time I was twelve years old work was my occupation, my religion, my recreation, my life. I was in my third year of high school, and as I had already skipped a year, my classmates at the convent school were thirteen. I was a ferocious student with a strongly competitive spirit. In spite of my dedication I wasn't interested in learning for its own sake. I was determined to make something of myself in the world *so my father would be proud of me*. I determined to make him happy to have sired a daughter instead of a son.

My schedule was staggering. My first class began at 8:00 A.M., and school wasn't finished for the day until 6:00 P.M. During this time students had a half-hour lunch break, another thirty minutes for recreation, and, late in the day, fifteen minutes for a snack. Students were allowed to converse with each other only during these breaks, which were denied if we broke the rules. I didn't resent these strict rules, perhaps because my life at home was even more confining.

I reached home at six-thirty every evening, and for the next two hours I did my homework and studied languages. My dinner was served at eight-thirty, an early hour in Spain, where adults of my parents' class didn't dine until eleven. After I ate I returned to work for at least two more hours. I followed this regimen six days and nights each week.

It was important that I stand at the top of my class. My father demanded it, and even more important, I set it as a self-imposed standard. Students were graded and ranked weekly, and I think I would have been ashamed and afraid to go home had I ranked lower than third in any subject.

My father often told me I was intelligent, which I already knew, and he never let me forget that I was fortunate to be given the best of all possible educations. It was my obligation to take full advantage of these opportunities. I not only believed him at the time, but I am still convinced he was right.

This may be hard to accept, but I was not brainwashed. Thanks to my battles with the governess, I had developed a mind of my own. Whenever I was given an order I analyzed it, and if I agreed with it I obeyed. If I thought it was foolish or irrelevant, or if I disagreed with it, I promptly tried to find ways to avoid it.

One example will explain what I mean. By the time I was twelve I no longer believed in the teachings or theology of the Roman Catholic church. My parents ordered me to attend mass every morning before school, but I refused to go at any time. My mother argued and cajoled, threatened and begged, but I resisted with such stubborn force that she finally gave up, and so did my father.

So I am telling a simple truth when I say that I studied because I wanted to learn. And another simple truth: I wanted to make my father happy.

In June, at the end of that school year, my father called me into his office to tell me he was proud of me. This was the first time he had ever praised me, but he qualified his remarks. I had ranked first in four of my subjects, and he said that the following year he expected me to lead my class in all six.

Then he had a surprise in store for me. He said he was leaving a few days later for a month's tour of the electric companies he owned, and he intended to take me with him. I would inspect his companies with him, see how business was conducted, and learn how hard an executive had to fight in order to achieve results.

I was wildly excited as I packed my suitcase, but I remembered to take my schoolbooks with me. After all, I had to gain a head start for the next term.

For the next four weeks my father and I traveled constantly—by car, on foot, on horseback or donkey. We inspected electrical lines, dams and hydroelectric plants; we talked with plant managers and workers, and we studied ledgers. The pace was grueling, but only once did I complain. My father's eyes became icy as he asked, "What do I have for a child, a delicate flower or an Agustina de Aragon?"

Agustina was a Spanish national heroine, our Joan of Arc, who had defended the city of Zaragoza from the French armies of Napoleon in 1802. I wanted to be an Agustina, tough and strong and courageous, so I had to display a consistent attitude. I did henceforth.

I spent hours walking through plants until my legs were ready to give way. I didn't yawn as I listened to long welcoming speeches by fat mayors, and I soon learned that the louder and longer the welcome, the more a town owed my father in electric bills. I had a very small appetite, and I soon developed a technique of cutting my enormous portions at the nightly banquets into tiny pieces to disguise my inability to eat more than token amounts of food. Above all, I learned to distinguish between glib flattery and genuine admiration. And by the time our tour ended I knew appearances meant nothing, that only hard work achieved satisfactory results.

That trip changed my relations with my father. After we came home, he formed the habit of discussing business with me every Sunday, and often on warm evenings I accompanied him on long walks. He talked about every aspect of his business and used me as a sounding board for his own ideas. I always listened carefully, never interrupted, and I learned how to profit from the mistakes of others.

Before I was awarded my secondary school diploma at the age of sixteen I also attended a business college at night. This double study routine exhausted me for the only time in my life, and I was sent to the Costa del Sol for a month of swimming and sunning. I recuperated quickly and gained four pounds. By the time I returned I was ready to resume a sixteen-hour-a-day schedule.

At eighteen I finished business school with the equivalent of a master's degree. At twenty I won a master's in philosophy and letters at the university. But I am getting ahead of my story.

To put it mildly, my parents were the most conflict-ridden, incompatible couple I have ever known, and to this day, after nearly fifty years of marriage, there has been little or no change in their relationship. My father was an ambitious businessman, and money was his god. My mother thought of herself as spiritual, and no one in the family ever mentioned money in her presence.

That was only the beginning. She enjoyed classical music, while he liked popular music. She was deeply religious, while he attended mass only because he thought it might be bad for business if he weren't seen at church. Mama was generous, often visiting the sick and poor, but Papa was a cynic who believed life dealt people their just rewards and punishments. My mother loved my sister, to the extent that she cared for anyone, but was indifferent toward me. My father was proud of me, although he rarely showed it, but my sister bored him because her mind was ordinary. Mama's taste in decorating, art and clothes was exquisite. Papa's taste was atrocious, and we were always apprehensive whenever he presented a member of the family with a gift, because we knew the recipient would be obliged to wear or use it, or run the risk of offending him.

With all this at work, I reached puberty having sworn to myself that I would never marry. I didn't want to take the chance of living with an incompatible husband. At thirteen I became aware of sex and my resolve wavered. A good-looking young man, many years my senior, who was a friend of an older cousin, came to visit us one day, and I discovered the pleasant game of touching his knees with mine beneath the dining table. He paid no attention to me, and I was crushed.

A long time passed before I came in contact with any other young men. My parents were worse than old-fashioned; their approach was simply Islamic, and under no circumstances would a young suitor have been welcome under their roof. I saw only girls at the convent school, of course, and at no time did I as much as exchange greetings with a teen-aged boy.

Thanks to the movies, I was able to have the film stars of the era as the men in my frequent erotic dreams. Most often I dreamed about Rock Hudson.

Then I discovered real men—the handsome, uniformed army officers who paraded, strutted and strolled up and down Madrid's broad avenues. I flirted with them crudely, frequently and outrageously, and to my chagrin they totally ignored the schoolgirl in pigtails. But that didn't stop me from thinking about what they carried between their legs. In the Prado and other museums I had seen many statues of nude men—poor substitutes for the real thing, but my imagination was lively.

At last, when I was sixteen, I met a young diplomat with dark, fiery eyes at a little party given by a friend of mine. I believed him to be unofficially engaged to another friend, but that didn't stop me from smiling and batting my eyelashes at him. It must have been my ingenuousness that interested him, and the next day he telephoned me.

For the sake of Isabel, my friend, I righteously refused to have anything to do with him, but he quickly assured me that Isabel was in love with a friend of his, not with him. So much for my scruples.

The immediate problem was how to arrange a date alone with him. I had a governess who was permanently glued to me, escorting me to and from school every day, accompanying me to the movies, staying close beside me when I went shopping. My parents believed in the old

Spanish custom of providing a girl with a chaperone, and I had no choice in the matter. But the diplomat, who was wiser than I in the ways of the world, promised he would attend to the chaperone.

The following day he arrived with a magnificent alligator handbag as a gift for her, and casually told her where and when to meet us. To my astonishment, she agreed.

On our first date I was very demure, and it required no effort to act the role of the shy virgin, because that's what I was. As he drove through our neighborhood I kept ducking my head and sat low in my seat so no one I knew could see me driving unchaperoned with a man. He headed out to the suburbs, and it became somewhat easier for me to chat. But I was distracted by his fiery glances, literally searing into me every time he looked at me. I controlled myself, however, and played the perfect lady.

By our third date I cast aside all restraints and peeled off my blouse so he could admire my small breasts, which were regarded in Spain as more attractive than breasts that resembled balloons. He was startled, of course, finding it hard to believe that a girl with my background could behave like a wanton. That didn't stop him from doing what came naturally to him, however.

In the weeks that followed, Jose and I knew many pleasures with each other. He was an experienced, expert teacher and I was a very willing pupil. We did everything except engage in actual intercourse, from which both of us held back. I was impulsive and perhaps foolish, but I had enough sense to know that no man of stature would marry me if I lost my virginity. And Jose, a proud Spaniard, could not entertain the notion of facing my father if I became pregnant.

I was growing up, passing from girlhood to womanhood, and Jose was so much on my mind that I found it difficult to concentrate on my work. One day I wanted him so desperately that I cut my classes at business school to visit his house, and I begged him to take me. He had the good sense to refuse, and I was furious with him—for a short time—believing he loved me less than I loved him.

Sometimes we spoke of marriage after I reached adulthood. I didn't realize it at the time, but my "love" for Jose was inspired, at least in part, by a sense of rebellion against my parents. My friends and classmates were permitted to stay out unchaperoned until ten o'clock and were permitted to go to dances, parties and movies with boys. But not I.

I have no idea what might have developed in my romance with Jose had we gone on together without interruption. But that was not to be, because the inevitable happened: A friend of my parents saw me riding alone with Jose in his car and duly reported this shocking fact.

My father went wild. He roared, fumed, exploded, raved and cursed. It was the only time in my life I've ever seen him lose his temper, and neither before nor after the day of our scene have I heard him use such language. I was terrified, and by the time he was through with me I was reduced to a quivering pulp.

I was forbidden to see Jose again, and it was made very clear to me that if I disobeyed I'd be thrown out of the house. My sympathetic governess was discharged, and was replaced that same day by a female Teutonic drill sergeant who made my original German governess appear warm and loving.

To say that my relations with my family were strained is a gross understatement; they were virtually nonexistent. My father walked past me without seeing me, and spoke to me only on Sunday afternoons, when he continued to discuss business with me. The world might fall apart, but nothing was allowed to interfere with business.

My mother was angry, restless and impatient. She wept hysterically, insisting I had "tarnished" my reputation. Then she pounded at me with a question she repeated daily, "Are you unwell," I swore to her that I was still a virgin, but it was obvious she didn't believe me, and for the first time I could remember she paid attention to me, keeping me under such constant observation that I wanted to scream.

Even my sister was forbidden to have anything to do with me, apparently because my parents were afraid my wickedness might rub off on her. The poor girl's spirit had been broken much earlier in life, and she obeyed meekly.

For months I lived in a strange limbo, spending virtually all of my waking hours at my studies. I was allowed to go nowhere, see no one and do nothing but work. I ate dinner with the adults now, and my evenings at the ornately laid table were a special form of torture.

My father, the most pessimistic human being I have ever known, held forth at great length as he discussed the disasters that were about to befall everyone he knew.

He himself was on the verge of bankruptcy, and all of our property, including our house, furniture and belongings, would be snatched from him at any moment. I knew enough of his business affairs to realize these prophecies of gloom had no foundation. On the contrary, he had never made as much money, and his financial position was unassailable.

I lacked the courage to tell him his claims of pending doom were preposterous. I was already in enough trouble, so I sat at the table in complete silence.

My mother contributed to the evening's gaiety by discussing in full detail the latest of her imaginary illnesses. She had developed severe hypochondria and never tired of talking about her latest ailment—usually a rare disease about which modern medicine knew little. I was already playing a private game, looking up these diseases in a medical encyclopedia, and I often wondered where she acquired her information about them.

My father either paid no attention to her incessant complaints or became annoyed. I sat with downcast eyes while she droned on, but I had to listen to her. If my mind wandered she knew it, and I was treated to a fresh tirade about the uncaring, callous lost sheep of the family.

My poor, beautiful sister never spoke, either. I would have given anything to look like her, but she was a tormented soul. She was placid by nature, and my father had told her frequently that her mind was inferior to mine, so she was riddled with feelings of inadequacy, particularly in my presence.

We were not the most joyous of families, but the worst was still to come. My beloved Jose, who was something of a playboy, finally went too far. He had an affair with a lovely young woman who was married to his cousin, and the husband, finding them in bed together, picked up a gun and shot Jose in the arm.

The police were called in, the newspapers played up the scandal for all it was worth, and the trio became the talk of Madrid. The husband was absolved because he had committed a "justified crime of passion." The Foreign Ministry banished Jose to a remote post in East Africa, where the mosquitoes and other insects did their best to devour him.

That was the end of the matter for everyone but my father. Every night he delivered the same lecture. The adulterous wife was beneath contempt. Jose was an unprincipled Don Juan. The husband was an impetuous fool. And I was an abandoned creature for having associated with such depraved aristocrats. The fact that I scarcely knew the husband and wife was irrelevant.

The scandal broke my heart. My one true love had been faithless, turning from me to a married woman, and I grieved. No one can suffer as badly as a romantic, sixteen-year-old girl, and my sorrow was unbearable. I spent most of my time in my room, weeping, sulking and proclaiming my misery.

One day my mother told me I should be ashamed of myself. Whether her words influenced me I don't know, but my reflection in the mirror sickened me. I was hollow-eyed, my face was gaunt and my cream-colored complexion had turned a sickening green.

"In one week," I told her, "I will put the whole matter out of my mind, and I'll be fine again."

That is precisely what happened. I had learned to

exert willpower when I concentrated on my studies, and now I applied the same inner techniques to my emotional state. I willed myself to forget Jose, and I did. I was completely, permanently cured, and was ready for new adventures.

In spite of my parents' attempts to confine me in a hothouse, I was introduced to any number of young men. I had friends of my own age, classmates and the daughters of people my parents knew, and I was often invited to their homes. Since they were living in the middle of the twentieth century, young men were permitted to call on them, and I met many.

Some were charming, some were handsome and a few were intelligent, but none interested me. The circumstances of my meetings with them simply didn't create a romantic atmosphere.

One day during the following year, when I was seventeen, I went to the horse races accompanied by my ever-present governess, and there, by prearrangement, I met two girls whom I knew well. Both had dates.

One of these men was a lawyer, many years older than I, a man who was an expert in the art of flirtation. He didn't leave my side all afternoon, and by the time the races ended I imagined myself wildly in love with him.

If I hadn't gone to the races that day I might not have met Juan. Certainly I had no idea that meeting him would change and influence my entire life.

Three

It was easy for me to arrange to see Juan alone, without the knowledge of my governess. I was a student at the university, and although I was escorted to and from school, my days were my own. So Juan was able to meet me on the campus, and we either strolled together or sat on a grassy slope and discussed life and love. Mostly love.

The second time we were together he told me he loved me, and naturally I believed him; I thought I was in love with him as well. I was too inexperienced and naïve to realize we scarcely knew each other. At our first meeting I convinced myself that I fell madly in love with him, and that conviction continued to grow.

Juan was a Basque, and after my childhood experiences in the north I should have known how difficult it would be for me to establish a rapport with a member of a group I regarded as dour, crude and alien. He was a highly ambitious lawyer, and I would have believed the friends who might have told me, but didn't, that he knew my family background and was interested in me because of the help my father could provide in Juan's career.

It didn't cross my mind that Juan was offering me a chance to escape from the disciplines and restrictions of life under my parents' roof. In reality he was a stranger. I knew nothing about his mind, his personality, his likes and dislikes. It was enough that he held my hand when we sat on the grass, that he kissed me when we went for drives in his car. It was enough that I persuaded myself that I loved him. I wanted him to take me to bed, to possess me completely, and I thought of little else.

I was a romantic teen-age innocent who became obsessed with sex. I could think only how wonderful it would be if Juan made love to me. I made no secret of my desire when I was with him, and he handled me with the expertise of a gifted misanthrope, kissing and caressing me while always stopping short of what I demanded.

He drove me wild, which was his intention. I could no longer concentrate on my studies, and I believed I would go mad if we weren't married soon. Juan encouraged me, speaking incessantly of the pleasures we would enjoy when we were married.

I lied to my parents without a qualm. I was going to spend an extra hour or two at the library; I had to confer with a professor; I was going horseback riding. He carried on an unrelenting campaign of love. I was alive only when I was with Juan, and he played on my infatuation. When he proposed I accepted before the words were out of his mouth.

But we needed my father's consent because I was a minor and I was afraid to talk to Papa. When I begged him to elope with me he refused, insisting that because of his respect for me he wanted us to be married in the "right" way. I didn't dream that because he was a lawyer he was aware of the consequences of making love to a minor, or that his real aim was the improvement, through my family, of his vocational and social standing. Under no circumstances did he want to antagonize my father, whom he hadn't yet met.

I procrastinated for a month, dreaming of the ecstasy that would be mine. Juan and I would spend all of our waking hours making love. And I would be free! No longer would I be required to obey my parents' unending rules! I would be the mistress of my own home, a woman who could do as she pleased! The very idea of such unaccustomed liberty made me giddy.

Occasionally, I must admit, I was sufficiently sensible to wonder how a mature, experienced man in his thirties could have fallen in love so completely and so rapidly with a girl of seventeen who knew nothing about the world. Then I looked in the mirror and dismissed my doubts. How could Juan fail to love such a radiant girl?

I daydreamed so constantly that my father finally became aware of my indisposition and demanded to know if I was lazy. I told him I had to speak to him on a matter of urgent importance. Now I was trapped, and couldn't delay any longer.

My father took me to his library-study, where all serious discussions were held. I looked into his cold, unyielding eyes and poured out my whole story.

My father was silent until I ran out of words. Then he told me I was a *mocosa,* a small child, and banished me to my room. My new governess was dismissed, and was replaced by yet another, who didn't let me out of her sight. I no longer had any alternative, and was compelled to study for my final examinations, which was fortunate, as I passed them with honors.

A short time later the family went to the Costa del Sol for the summer. A few hours after our arrival I went into the pine woods so I could daydream about my lost love, and there my mother joined me. I began to babble to her about Juan.

"Adela," she said, "you are really in love."

I agreed, fervently, and her expression told me she was afraid of love.

"I hope," she said after hesitating, "you wouldn't go too far—and lose your purity."

My situation endowed me with a shrewdness I had never before possessed. I knew instantly that if I played on my mother's fear that I might lose my virginity, I would make her my ally. "I try very hard, Mama," I said, "but I'm afraid I am weak."

"Then," she replied, "you should be married immediately."

Not until much later did I understand that more than her concern for my virginity prompted her change of mind. I'm sure she herself didn't realize that here was an opportunity to be rid of a daughter whose presence at home gave her no joy.

She went to work at once, and was joined in her campaign by a pious cousin of my father's who was spending the summer with us. My father was stubborn, and our nightly dinners were stormy and uncomfortable, but the good ladies persisted, and finally he surrendered, giving his reluctant consent.

Again he took me into the library, and made a final attempt to change my mind. I was very young, and Juan was so much older that we had little in common. Furthermore he was a Basque, which meant he was rough, humorless and might be inclined to drink heavily. Also, Basques were like the Moors of old, and their wives led segregated lives. Papa's only logical conclusion was that a marriage to Juan would be certain to fail.

I replied I still wanted to marry Juan, and that nothing would change my mind.

My father lost his temper, banged on his desk with his fist and shouted that I was under his authority until I was twenty-one. He threatened to send me off to England to school unless I came to my senses.

I hurried off to my room so I could weep in private; at that stage of my life tears came easily.

Soon my mother joined me, and for the only time in our lives we enjoyed a close rapport. She assured me that my father stood alone, that everyone else in the family sympathized with me, particularly the women. My aunts and cousins, even my sister stood with me, and all of them were exerting pressure on my father.

He succumbed to that pressure, and again gave his consent, so the way was clear. Eventually he and Juan had a private talk, and at last I was to be married!

On the day before our engagement was announced, Juan gave me a lovely diamond bracelet, which I adored. It was the only jewelry I ever received from him.

My father pretended I didn't exist, which upset me badly, in spite of my happiness. On the day before the wedding he came to my room after the manicurist had left. He wanted to speak to me.

He told me he wouldn't object in the least if I didn't want to go through with the wedding, and that he would take care of all the details, including the return of wedding gifts. "Believe me," he said, "I will be the happiest man in the world if you'll do this."

One of the things that distressed him was my failure to obtain a signed pre-nuptial agreement from Juan, a contract of a type that was customary when the bride was a member of a family in our circumstances. As a matter of fact, I had mentioned such an agreement to Juan, who had been outraged by the suggestion. He had accused me of being materialistic, saying that in a true marriage the partners shared everything. He had sworn he intended to earn enough money to support me, and had urged me to leave all such matters in his hands. Looking back over the years, I felt uneasy because I never told my father about that conversation.

We followed Spanish custom to the letter. Juan paid for my white bridal gown, and my parents bought our furniture and household goods. One of my greatest, life-long faults has been my habitual tardiness, and I arrived at the church for my wedding an hour late. Most of the guests had long faces, and so did the bridegroom, who was wearing new shoes that pinched his feet.

I had engaged all kinds of "artists" to make me up, comb and dress my hair, fix my wedding veil, and in their typical fashion, they all worked very slowly and methodically and talked incessantly. I was dressed all in white, with sprigs of lilies of the valley tucked into my hair and in a small bridal bouquet. My father escorted me down the aisle to join Juan who was accompanied by his sister.

After the religious ceremony we signed the civil marriage papers in the sacristy and then returned to my parents' house for the reception, which was attended by five hundred people.

My father loaned us his car and chauffeur, and Juan and I started off for a honeymoon on the Spanish and French Riviera, to be followed by a stay on the island of Majorca. I was ecstatic.

We left Madrid about seven-thirty in the evening and drove on poor country roads to Zaragosa, arriving late in the evening. Our hotel suite was filled with white flowers, and I went off to the bathroom to make myself beautiful. I spent a long time bathing and primping, and by the time I emerged Juan was sound alseep. My disappointment was acute.

The next day we went sight-seeing, and then—with our marriage still unconsummated—we drove on to Barcelona. All the passion that Juan had demonstrated in the weeks prior to our marriage had vanished, and I had the uneasy feeling that I bored him. I was too proud to ask him why he had become so indifferent to me, and had to keep looking in a mirror to assure myself I hadn't been transformed into an old witch. My reflection reassured me, and I wondered if something was wrong with Juan.

Finally, after we reached Barcelona, I summoned the courage to bring up the problem. He told me there was something bothering him: I looked too young to be a married woman.

I reminded him that I was only seventeen.

Juan replied that he couldn't make love to someone who looked like a child. Promising to take care of everything, he went out and bought me a chignon that made me look like Sarah Bernhardt, who had gone out of fashion many years earlier.

The chignon made me look ten years older, but Juan still wasn't satisfied. At last I resembled an adult, he said, but my clothes were those of a child, and I looked absurd in them. We went shopping, and he selected a new wardrobe for me, buying me dresses that would have been just right for my mother.

Our hotel suite was filled with flowers from relatives and friends, but there were none from Juan, and I began to feel annoyed. We seemed to have nothing to say to each other, and it was dawning on me that his conduct was bizarre.

He sank onto the huge bed, sighing deeply, and I thought this was my chance to break the ice. I sat close beside him, let my hair fall and tossed it coquettishly. Nothing happened.

"Aren't you going to make love to me?" I asked him.

"If a woman is intelligent," he said, "she never asks that question. She waits."

I jumped to my feet, so angry I began to shake. "Obviously, I don't appeal to you physically!"

"Nonsense," he said. "This is just one of those things that often happens. I'm not prepared."

I thought he was teasing me, and decided to play the same game. "All right, put your imagination to work. Imagine yourself alone in a bedroom with a redheaded girl—"

"I don't happen to like redheads."

"Okay," I said, "I'll dye my hair. Imagine me as a blonde."

"I don't care for blondes, either. They're too washed out."

My temper slipped. "You choose the color!"

There was a long, uneasy silence before Juan said, "Brunette. With olive skin."

I was exasperated. "My skin is too pale, and you know it!" I covered his eyes with my hands, still trying to humor him. "Very well, imagine that I'm a tall, svelte brunette who tears off her clothes."

His eyes were closed, and I pushed him backward onto the bed, then undressed as quickly as I could.

Juan opened his eyes, saw me naked beside him and grimaced. I swear he looked pained.

I would not be denied, however, and began to caress him. His eyes closed again, and soon he was breathing deeply, like someone who had fallen asleep. Even when I threw myself on top of him he made no move. In desperation I opened his trousers, and was bewildered when I realized he wasn't aroused.

I became hysterical. I jumped to my feet, examined myself critically in a full-length mirror and then kissed my reflection until I became exhausted. Then I threw myself into a chair and slumped there for hours.

At last Juan stirred and opened his eyes.

I glared at him. "You fell asleep while I was making love to you," I said.

He had the gall to laugh.

In a fury I dashed into the bathroom and locked the door behind me. Juan pounded on the door for a long time, but I made no reply. Eventually I became calm enough to put on makeup for the evening, and when I finally came out I combed my hair and dressed in silence.

We exchanged few words at dinner.

I thought of a separation and wondered if I could get

an annulment. I wanted to call my father, but was so inexperienced that I was afraid. I had never discussed sex with my father, who had made it very plain to me that when one married, one stayed married. I decided I had to make the best of a bad situation.

During the following days we went sight-seeing, attended a bullfight and went shopping. Finally, on the sixth night of our marriage Juan tried to make love to me, but nothing happened.

The scene was repeated the next night, and I asked him what was wrong with him.

"With me?" he shouted. "With you! You have an impediment, a rare impediment!"

I was stunned, and began to weep.

"Go to see a doctor and have him take care of you before you come back to me," he said, and dropped off to sleep.

The next day we went to Majorca, where a villa that had been made available to us by friends of my family awaited us. Juan promptly launched me on an athletic program. We climbed mountains, we swam, played tennis, went bicycling and horseback riding until I was exhausted, and when I crept into bed at night Juan went off on his own.

By the time we flew to France my attitude had changed. I was still a virgin, and a virgin I wanted to remain. The very thought of making love with Juan sickened me. I was disillusioned, and our marriage had become a farce.

At Cannes I developed a new routine. Juan took a long nap after lunch every day, and while he slept I went sailing or swimming, and sometimes visited friends who were staying there. Had I been alone I would have enjoyed myself.

One day I returned to the hotel earlier than Juan expected me, and by mistake left the elevator one floor below our suite. Not until I approached the door did I realize my error. The door was open, and a man and woman were standing there, engaging in a low, intimate conversation. She was a brunette with olive skin.

My mind refused to register his identity until he turned and looked at me.

I fled, leaving the hotel and racing out into the open, afraid I would faint or become ill. I still don't know where I ran or how long I wandered around the strange city, but at last I came to a church. The main doors were locked, but I found a side door that was open, crept in and fell asleep on a pew.

It was morning when I awakened and left the church. My first thought was to return to Madrid while Juan stayed on with his mistress. But I didn't want to go back to my parents' home, where I would not only be imprisoned again but would be forced to listen to incessant criticism and snide remarks.

Ultimately I gained enough courage to go to a public telephone and make a long-distance call to my father. Instead of telling him the whole story I hesitated, finally revealing that I was unhappy.

My father exploded. I was immature and shameless, he told me. He refused to listen to my complaints, and after telling me my place was with my husband, he slammed down the telephone.

In my desolation I decided to move to another hotel

while I made my plans. I took a room, then paid a bell-boy to pick up my luggage.

To my astonishment Juan returned with him. He was charming, gallant and apologetic. The girl was not his mistress. She had picked him up in the bar, and he had escorted her to her door, but he hadn't gone to bed with her. He swore he was telling the truth.

Naturally, I didn't believe a word of his feeble story.

He begged me to return to our suite with him. Even then I didn't realize that his one aim was to remain on good terms with my father.

We argued for an hour, and I finally went with him because I had nowhere else to turn. I hated him.

We resumed our strange honeymoon, staying at arm's length from each other, speaking only when necessary.

A few days later a photo fell out of Juan's wallet, and when I picked it up I recognized the girl in the doorway. I finally realized that, in all probability, she had accompanied us on our entire trip.

I was so shocked I could neither eat nor sleep, and Juan cut short our honeymoon. The thought of annulment must have been very much in his mind and, as he would have lost everything he hoped to gain by our marriage, he wanted to make certain I could make no claim of virginity to an ecclesiastical or civilian court.

We spent the last night of our trip in Valencia, and there Juan took me. Violently, brutally and without feelings. I loathed him as I had never despised another human being.

When we reached Madrid we moved into a penthouse apartment my father had rented for us, and immediately went our separate ways. We met only in passing, exchanging a few curt words only when necessary. He had his marriage, and I had my freedom.

I busied myself with decorating the apartment, and then, when time began to hang on my hands, I returned to the university, where I began to study philosophy and literature. I resumed the patterns I had formed years earlier, but there was one difference. No restrictions were placed on me, and I could come and go as I pleased.

Gradually I became aware of men again, and when I felt in the mood I flirted with them, never feeling guilty. For the sake of appearances I sometimes went with Juan and his friends to nightclubs, and I realized for the first time that Juan had a serious drinking problem, just as my father had prophesied. Often he became so intoxicated that I slipped out and went home alone.

One weekend, when I went to a bridge party, my first beau, Jose, appeared and was seated at the next table. At best I'm bored by bridge, and my game that day was a disaster. Jose was as attentive to me as he had been when we had first met. I had been humiliated by my husband, I was lonely and starved for affection, and it was not difficult for Jose to convince me that he was still in love with me.

We saw each other frequently. Sometimes, when Juan became drunk at a nightclub, I telephoned Jose, who picked me up and took me home. I knew we wouldn't establish a permanent relationship, but a second-rate romance was better than none.

Juan must have sensed that I was slipping away from him. After two years of living apart under the same roof he sometimes forced himself on me, and ultimately I became pregnant.

Almost immediately after I learned I was going to have a baby, another crisis was brewing. The crass husband of a cousin of mine, a Frenchman whose advances I had rejected, went to Juan and told him I was engaged in an illicit romance.

Juan came to me and demanded the truth.

Only a nineteen-year-old girl who had been degraded and shamed as I had could have been so arch. "I've had a remarkable experience with the man you're asking about," I said. "We have flown together in a dream, and one is not conscious of what happens in dreams."

He slapped me across the mouth with the back of his hand and bellowed for the truth.

I was so angry I deliberately infuriated him by quoting Friedrich Nietzsche to him in Latin: *"Quidquid luce fruit, tenebris agit."* In other words, "Whoever escapes from the light gets darkness."

That philosophical observation coming from a young girl showing off her intellectual superiority was more than he could tolerate. He beat me severely. I screamed accusations of his moral degeneracy at him and taunted him with the happiness Jose had been able to give me instead.

The Spain of the early 1950s was still a backward country where women held second-class citizenship, and I could do nothing on my own initiative. I had two choices. The first was that of going to Jose, and I could imagine the scandal. I was wise enough to realize that Jose would have fled had a married woman of nineteen, carrying her husband's baby, come to him for protection.

The more sensible move was to go to my father,

which I did, and he offered me his complete support because he felt the honor of our family had been stained. I made no mention of Jose, and it was enough for my father that his pregnant daughter had been beaten by her brute of a husband.

My father's one idea was that I should leave the country until Juan and I both calmed down and our marriage could be patched. It did not occur to him that I was determined never to see Juan again, never to have anything to do with him.

I refrained from expressing myself. My father was making all the necessary arrangements for me to go to England, and I wanted nothing to disturb those plans.

A few days later I was on an airplane, headed for London. Juan knew I was leaving, but assumed I would return after a short time. Spain had strict laws limiting the amount of money one could take out of the country, so Juan felt certain I'd be obliged to come back after a short time abroad.

I had no intention of returning, but I had no idea that I was completely turning my back on the only world, the only way of life, I had ever known. Many years would pass before I would go back to Spain.

Four

In London I was a stranger in an alien land, but I lost no time looking for work, and soon found a place in an advertising agency, where my knowledge of languages was useful. I lived on the money my father had given me and saved every penny of my salary. I made it my business to become friendly with an American who worked at the agency, and convinced him I had an urgent need for a visa. He had friends at the United States embassy, and it didn't take long to get my visa.

I sold some of my jewelry so I could buy a first-class ticket on the *Queen Elizabeth*. I was still accustomed to high living, but I had a private reason for wanting to travel in style. I understood instinctively that the right connections are important to success, and my hunch was right. On board the ship I met people who told me where to live and how to get along; also, they provided me with introductions to many people.

I'm still not certain when I made up my mind that I would settle in the United States, and I may not have made the decision consciously or deliberately. Like so many immigrants, I simply knew that the future held more promise for me there than anywhere else. Never would I return to Juan, never could I live with my parents. To set up a home for myself elsewhere in Spain was out of the question. The struggle would be too hard in England or France; both countries were struggling to reestablish their economies after the difficult years of World War II.

I knew America would be my home, and I have never regretted my move.

I took a small, inexpensive room at a "good" address, accepted a number of social engagements and began to look for business opportunities. I had changed my tourist visa into a business visa, but I couldn't take a paying job, nevertheless there were other, legitimate ways to earn money, and I scoured the newspapers daily, searching for ideas.

Meanwhile I developed an active social life, warning myself that as a foreigner I had to behave circumspectly at all times. Americans could unbend, but I was an outsider, and therefore had to be above suspicion.

It was difficult to keep my resolve. Everyone I met, it seemed, wanted to talk about only two subjects, the evils of Franco's Spain and the evils of the Spanish Inquisition. I felt like the defendant at a trial, and—maintaining a surface calm—I had to go to great lengths to convince my new acquaintances that I was the least prejudiced person in New York. Once they relaxed, I felt more at ease.

After two weeks I concluded that the mail-order business was the right approach. But I learned at the post office that I couldn't advertise until I had merchandise in hand, and my capital was very limited.

Then I went to a lawyer I had met socially.

He told me I could start a simple company by registering it with the city of New York for ten dollars. He also told me his exorbitant fee, but indicated he would waive it if I went to bed with him. I fled that office.

That visit taught me a lesson. A woman who is young and wants to make her way in the business world must look attractive, but under no circumstances should she make herself overly attractive. She should dress quietly, make up discreetly and behave modestly. Otherwise she'll wind up as someone's mistress, and soon will open a boutique. If she's lucky it will be on Madison Avenue; if not, she'll find herself in the Bronx. And either way she won't be in business for long. The mortality rate of mistress-operated boutiques is high.

My experience with the lawyer also taught me another lesson: I had been wrong to mix business and pleasure. I swore to myself that I would earn my living on one level, but would keep my social life apart. I kept that promise until I met the man who is now my husband. So much for high resolves.

I opened my mail-order business, buying small quantities of inexpensive merchandise and replenishing my stock out of profits. Never in my life had I earned a penny, but I remembered everything I had heard in Papa's Sunday afternoon lectures. Everything he had said came back to me, and I tried to apply his principles to my tiny business.

I was not surprised when I found I could earn a modest living for myself. My father was a cold, harsh man, but I had complete confidence in his talents as a businessman, and my faith was soon justified. My work offered me no security, and I was unable to accumulate any capital, but at least I was earning my way.

I analyzed my situation, as I have since done many times over the years, and came to the conclusion that in order to produce imaginatively in business one needs peace of mind. I mean both physical and metaphysical peace, as well as a degree of financial security.

But all that had to wait. Five months after I landed in New York my son was born, and I named him Carlos. I was alone in the hospital, and knew no one well enough to have any visitors. This isolation made me realize I was dependent on myself, but I refused to become terrified.

When I was released from the hospital I reorganized my routines. I had already taken a small apartment for my son and myself, and my mail-order business kept me at home, which was all to the good. I found a reliable baby-sitter who would take charge when I went out, and realized my parents would be horrified if they knew what I was doing. Although it didn't yet occur to me, I was already becoming Americanized.

That process was aided by my first real American friendship.

Bob was a happy young man, an extrovert who seemed rarely to suffer inner doubts, was honest, plain and forthright, and at the beginning of our relationship his one desire was to conquer me. A goal he never achieved. I'm sure that throughout our friendship he continued to hope, because I fascinated him, but he was unable to invade my private world. I learned much about the American character from him, though, and enjoyed our friendship while it lasted.

The need for a steady income led me to accept a position with a Seventh Avenue company that made knitted goods. By this time I had applied to the Immigration and Naturalization Service for a change in my status, but it hadn't yet materialized, so I was still forbidden to accept a salary. I was hired to supervise the work of the Spanish-speaking machine operators, and in return I was to be paid a commission, based on sales.

I arrived early each morning and spent the whole day on the job. My hours became increasingly long because my employer asked for more and more help; I was agreeable, believing it was important that I learn something about an American business. At the end of the month I asked for my money, but was told I'd have to wait until the company was paid by its clients.

I spent another month there, then went into my employer's office after the staff had left for the day and again asked to be paid. He replied by trying to rape me.

I screamed, and as the elevator was no longer running, ran down the stairs; like Cinderella, I lost one of my shoes.

After I reached the street I spent at least a quarter hour trying to compose myself. I was a mess; my hair and dress were disordered. I had only one shoe and had left my handbag in the office, but I had no intention of returning for it; I was therefore penniless.

It was raining, and the passersby, hurrying home after work, paid no attention to me. I continued to stand, unable to weep, totally immobilized, and by seven-thirty the garment district was deserted. I took off my one shoe, walked to Madison Avenue and boarded a bus. I asked another passenger for the fifteen-cent fare, but she replied that she had no change. So I got off, boarded another bus and this time was more fortunate; another woman saw that I was badly disturbed, and paid my fare.

My baby was asleep by the time I reached home, so I dismissed the sitter for the night and threw myself onto my bed. Was I too naïve and idealistic? Was my attitude too trusting for the hard-boiled New World? Or was I creating my own problems by dressing and making up provocatively? All I knew for certain was that I had wasted two months of my time and effort.

That night I went through one of the worst crises I had ever endured. Gradually my thoughts began to make sense, and I developed a determination to order my future. I was intelligent and had both the willingness and desire to work. Even more important, I knew I had the ability to produce creatively in business. As to my personal appearance, I knew I would be foolish if I failed to use my physical assets judiciously and to my advantage.

The next morning, carrying Carlos in my arms because I couldn't afford to buy a carriage, I returned to the Immigration and Naturalization Service office to ask for a complete list of the types of work I was permitted to accept. I learned there was no restriction on my employment by agencies and departments of foreign governments.

I looked up every consulate-general in New York City and, still carrying my baby, began to make the rounds. Finally, on the verge of giving up, I received an offer from the Argentine Purchasing Mission, which had offices in the Savoy Plaza Hotel. The salary was two hundred dollars per month, which wasn't much, even in the early 1950s, but it would provide me with a steady income—and an opportunity to learn.

I can best describe my position as that of an assistant clerk. The employees were efficient, far better than I at both typing and filing. At the end of my first week I decided I would need another avenue to promotion.

There were two executives in the office. One was an exceptionally able administrator, who needed no help. The other was a colonel who had received a political appointment from the Argentine government. He knew little about the business, but seemed eager to learn and worked hard. Soon I noticed that he was already in his office when the staff reported for work, so I began to appear earlier each morning, finally coming in at seven-thirty. The colonel was newly arrived in the United States, and also was handicapped by an inadequate command of English.

Developing our relationship slowly and subtly, I—an immigrant of a few months—began to advise him on American customs and manners. Ultimately I also managed to suggest to him that I might be helpful to him as an interpreter in his meetings with Americans.

Soon he took me with him to his meetings, and I began to keep notes on American companies, as well as on the executives I met. As I became more efficient and learned what the Americans expected, I took over more and more of the colonel's work, even correcting his errors without first checking with him.

As I had hoped, I was given a promotion to the position of his assistant, and my salary was raised to a respectable six hundred dollars per month, enough to enable me to support my baby and myself without worry. For the first time since I had come to the United States I stood on solid financial ground. As for the colonel, he soon took to long lunches and falling asleep afterward on the couch in his office.

At last I could look ahead, and I felt I was wasting precious work time by going home at four o'clock, when my day at the office ended. After thinking of the possibilities that might be open to me, I applied for a job at the United Nations as a translator. They told me that what was required was simultaneous interpretation, and they were interested in me because I was fluent in French and German as well as in Spanish and English.

I practiced at home for three months, then took a test at the UN and was hired. At my request I worked on the night shift, which enabled me to keep my day job at the Argentine Purchasing Mission. My income more than doubled, and I was able to save money.

During my lunch hour I worked on a project of my own, keeping a complete file on everyone I met in business, as well as maintaining exhaustive files on American corporations with which I dealt. At the same time I enlarged my circle of acquaintances at the UN, and came to know a number of diplomats fairly well.

I was a good listener, thanks to the enforced silence I had endured at home as a child and an adolescent. And I trained myself to remember anything I heard that might be useful. I learned, too, how to show off the knowledge I was acquiring. After all, I had no grandmother or aunt in America to publicize my talents for me.

One day a shipowner from California was surprised by my working knowledge of his business, and asked me to remain behind after a meeting. He asked me if I still had good connections in Spain. I assured him I did, and that I also had them in Belgium, the Netherlands, England and other countries.

He wanted to make contact with the Spanish government, and promised me a commission if I could help him put his deal together. He wanted enough capital to build ships in Japan, and hoped to interest Spain in the project.

I had already made it a habit to read the financial pages of the newspapers, so I knew there was a surplus of rice in Spain. I suggested to the shipowner that he use commodites as collateral, in this case to offer Spanish-owned rice to the Japanese. In this way he could secure the cash for his Japanese shipbuilding program. Meanwhile I would try to obtain a ten-year credit to pay the Spanish government for the rice.

Before I started to work on the project I asked the shipowner for a letter that would guarantee my commission if I was successful. He was upset, and told me his word was good.

"I don't doubt your word," I said, "but what about your memory?"

I got the letter, and went to work. During the next five months I exchanged innumerable letters with the Spanish government, and was ultimately successful.

When the whole deal was concluded about eight months later, I received a huge commission, and gained prestige on Wall Street and in shipping circles as well.

I wondered how to invest my money, and went to friends for advice. A number of them suggested the stock market, but I didn't care for the idea. It seemed to me that the market was controlled by large corporations, mutual funds and foundations, making it impossible for the small investor to control his own money. I began to search for something more solid.

Wherever I went I made notes, and I inquired about municipal developments in New York. Soon I learned that the Third Avenue elevated train demolition plans had been approved. Third Avenue would be redeveloped, and eventually Second Avenue would have a subway system.

I thought I would be wise to buy some small buildings on Second and Third Avenues. I did, and soon was the owner of four. Two were bargains, costing me eight thousand dollars in cash, but arranging for the mortgage of seventeen thousand dollars was tricky. My income from my Argentine and UN jobs didn't satisfy the banks, so I had to persuade friends to cosign the notes. After all the arrangements were made I found myself with four houses. The rental they brought in left me, after paying off the notes, interest and taxes, with three thousand dollars per year clear profit. I knew, too, that after redevelopment I would be able to sell those properties for a very large profit.

I was on my way, but still had no specific long-range plans for making money. Instead I tried to follow certain principles:

1. Work hard, and never waste time.

2. Be tenacious. Patience in business is a real virtue.

3. Be flexible. Don't specialize in any one field, but keep watch for opportunities. When certain that one is sound, seize it.

4. Diversify. Don't insist on doing just one thing,

when for whatever the reasons, an opportunity to do something else comes along.

By the end of 1955 my balance sheet had become favorable. No longer the penniless immigrant, I was beginning to prosper. But I still had a great deal to learn. Acting on the advice of a friend, I gambled on some Canadian gold stock, buying a few thousand shares at four cents per share. One day I learned the stock had jumped to forty cents.

I searched for my certificates, and discovered I had misplaced them. Each night I looked for the certificates, becoming increasingly frantic, because I was afraid the stock might fall as fast as it had gone up. It rose to fifty cents per share, then sixty cents, and still I couldn't find the certificates. By this time little Carlos and I had a young poodle, and I half convinced myself the puppy had chewed it up, and I was ready to tear the whole house apart to find the documents, or whatever might be left of them.

Finally, after devoting an entire Sunday to the hunt, I found the certificates wedged behind the television set. I sold the stock on Monday morning, and made a handsome profit. Later that week the government opened an investigation of the company, and the stock plummeted; anyone who still held it lost money.

This experience, from which I luckily escaped unhurt, taught me some lessons I should have known. Thereafter I never bought a stock until I had studied the balance sheets and knew something about the company and its operations, as well as its management.

By the end of 1956 I had broadened my contacts and my investments considerably. Without a single blink of my false eyelashes, I could discuss high markups, depletion allowances, credit consortiums, prime rates and investment tax credits. I was taking a graduate course in economics and finance from successful businessmen, and I perfected the fine art of listening.

Being a woman was an asset, and the fact that men found me attractive made my self-education still easier. Sometimes, however, I had to bite my tongue. Most men regarded me as an ignoramus, and if I dared to interrupt when they spelled out fundamentals, they were insulted and said, "Let me finish." I taught myself never to interrupt.

Still looking for ways to make money, I decided to invest in options on small houses in Manhattan and Queens. In order to find bargains I did a great deal of walking, particularly on Manhattan's East Side between 79th and 89th streets. With luck, I could buy an option for eight hundred dollars, then sell it a month or two later and show a profit of from five hundred to a thousand dollars.

I also devised another way of making money. I would rent an apartment for two years, for example; buy furniture at clearance sales and then sublet the place at a substantial profit to some temporary official assigned to the United Nations. During a period of one year I rented, furnished and sublet five apartments in the vicinity of the UN, and earned an income of twelve thousand dollars from the enterprise.

It required a special effort to find the time for these ventures. I looked at apartments and rented them on Saturdays, then signed the leases during lunch hours. On Sunday mornings I rested, but a new occupation kept me busy on Sunday afternoons. I translated copy into Spanish for an advertising agency, and soon I tried my hand at writing copy in return for a percentage of sales. One of my ads was quite successful, and my royalties provided me with additional income.

Early in the winter of 1958 there was a shakeup at the Argentine Purchasing Mission. The administrator and my colonel were recalled, and one of the office managers took over as the chief. He immediately issued an order to the effect that only Argentinians would be employed. There was only one foreigner on the payroll, and she left that same day.

To an extent, I knew my own conduct had been responsible. I had been so busy on behalf of the colonel that others in the office resented me and were jealous of me. Thanks to my aristocratic European upbringing, I had always kept my distance from others in the office, and as I had kept myself busy on various personal projects during my spare time, too, they thought me haughty. One other factor played a part in my discharge, and there was nothing I could have done about it. The man who took command was one of those males endowed with an overabundance of machismo, and he could not tolerate the presence of a woman who knew as much or more than he did.

So I was out. I wasn't worried about finding other work, but I still felt guilty and unhappy. I wasn't accustomed to being fired, and the experience was unsettling. That night, as I thought about what had happened, I realized the new head of the Argentine Mission had done me a favor. I had held the job too long, regarding it as my security base, and I was confident I could use my time to better advantage. Immobility, I told myself, could destroy me.

I began to search for a new business, and found it almost by accident. A girl I knew had rented me her old car for fifty dollars a month so I would have transportation to the outskirts of New York, where I hunted for low-income houses on which I could buy options. By this time I had learned to communicate with working people as well as financiers, and one day a chat with an attendant at a service station where I bought my gasoline opened a new door.

I told him I was looking for investment opportunities, and he gave me the card of a man who bought old automobiles, had them repainted and then shipped them to South America for resale. This man wanted to expand his business, and needed contacts in Chile and Peru, which I was in a position to supply, thanks to my UN friendships.

I checked the man's rating, found he was sound and made an appointment with him. First I inspected his workshop to assure myself that his business was legitimate. Then we talked for hours, and as a result of our discussion we decided to form a new corporation, in which he would own 60 percent of the stock and I would own 40 percent.

I jumped into the new enterprise with great enthusiasm, but I failed to take into account the snail's pace of business in South America. Some of the people to whom I wrote never bothered to reply, and it occurred to me that these Latins wanted nothing to do with a woman in business. So I began signing letters with my initial rather than my first name.

The pace increased very slightly, and my partner became impatient. On a number of occasions he telephoned me and said, "You sure gave me more words than business." I hated anyone to think of me as a phony, and I was furious, but I didn't know how to solve the problem.

I warned myself not to brood, and found an outlet for my emotions by taking my three-year-old son on my lap and speaking to him as though he were an adult. Gradually my vision cleared, and I knew I was insane to think I could establish a new business through correspondence alone.

I took a leave of absence from the United Nations, obtained an American passport for Carlos and went off for a tour of Venezuela, Colombia, Peru, Chile, Argentina and Brazil. I worked feverishly, saw dozens of people, and eventually made deals with two men to import second-hand cars. I took care to insure that I left functioning organizations behind me in both Colombia and Chile. These included a local partner, bookkeepers responsible to me, and a warehouse to store newly arrived cars.

I was tired when I returned to New York, my capital was almost exhausted and a nasty surprise awaited me in the form of a letter from my father, who hadn't bothered to communicate with me in any way for more than two years, even though I had written to him on many occasions.

He accused me of being a bad daughter, insensitive to my family and my country. Worst of all, I was a failure as a mother because I had left the security of home in order to eke out a precarious existence for my son and myself. This attack, which stunned me, was at complete odds with my view of myself. In my own eyes I was a heroine, struggling to make a good life for myself and Carlos in a strange land while being ignored by an indifferent family. My father concluded by saying I was a disgrace and that he would disinherit me if I did not return to Spain and my husband by the end of the month.

That letter was only the beginning of my troubles. Carlos was ill with intestinal flu. Only he knew, and he was too little to realize it, that I was no longer married to his father, having quietly obtained a divorce in the United States.

One final blow awaited me in the form of a brief letter from the Immigration and Naturalization Service. My visa had expired, and I was directed to leave the country.

I called one supposed friend, who said he knew nothing about immigration matters and couldn't help me.

My disgust cleared my mind. I had wanted freedom and had won it. Now, in spite of the threats to my financial and personal security, I was damned if I was going to lose everything I had fought so hard to achieve.

By dawn I had decided to go semi-underground and immediately went into action. Saying nothing to my landlord and leaving no forwarding address, I moved to a more obscure apartment, furnishing it with a few items I bought in a thrift shop. I used another of my multiple names, as most Spanish people have, in connection with my job at the UN, and got in touch with several friends, telling them I was leaving the country on an extended trip. I hadn't covered my tracks completely, but the immigration authorities, when they checked, did believe I had actually departed from the United States.

Meanwhile my job at the UN represented immediate security, and the second-hand car business I had just established in South America was my hope for the future. In the meantime I was an illegal alien who owned several houses but was desperately short of cash.

After I moved into the new apartment I felt more secure, and hoping to increase my income reinvested the rent I received from my Third Avenue properties by purchasing an old house in Queens. I talked a plumber into installing a new shower for one hundred dollars, and to save money I repainted the house myself. Carlos came with me every day, never complaining, and every afternoon we returned from Queens, weary and spattered with paint. I sold the house for a profit of thirty-eight hundred dollars.

I persuaded my partner in the used car business to have faith a little longer, and at the end of July, a month after my return, we received an order for twelve cars to be shipped to Valparaiso, Chile. We made a profit of $400 per car, and my share was $3,480. Each of us left $1,500 in the company and withdrew the rest.

Through my contacts at the UN I wrote scores of letters, and before long business was pouring in at a faster rate than we could handle. My partner and I decided to expand cautiously, hiring two mechanics to repair the old cars and another man to paint them.

Instinct taught me to follow certain procedures. I never dealt directly with the government of a South American republic because, in the event of an upheaval and the coming to power of another group, I didn't want our company to be accused of partisanship. Also, I was aware of the hatred so many Latin Americans felt for citizens of the United States. So, in my correspondence, I stressed my Spanish background and never mentioned my partner.

The business continued to grow. My financial gamble had paid off. But my troubles multiplied, too.

Five

My business interests were beginning to develop, and I was at last able to spend more time with my little son. But I was deeply disturbed, and nothing bothered me more than my perilous status as a stateless person. My Spanish passport had expired, and in those years could not be renewed without the consent of the man I had divorced. Spain doesn't recognize divorce, so under Spanish law I was still Juan's wife.

My growing business made it imperative that I return to South America, but if I tried to leave the United States I would be picked up by the American immigration authorities and wouldn't be allowed to return. I envied Carlos his American passport.

Each day I dreaded a pounding at the door that would result in my immediate deportation, and I became so afraid that I couldn't sleep. I had no intention of waiting for a miserable fate to overcome me and decided that something had to be done. I tried to take steps accordingly.

I telephoned a young man I knew, the son of a Senator who worked in his father's Washington office, and asked for his advice. He told me the Spanish immigration quota was small, and that the only way I could remain in the country was through the passage of a special bill through Congress. He promised to do what he could, but as the weeks passed it became painfully obvious that it wasn't possible to obtain enough support for my bill.

I was depressed and anxious, eager but unable to make another trip to South America. My dilemma was acute and I became somewhat reckless. To the best of my knowledge the immigration people had made no attempt to get in touch with me. So, with my affairs prospering, I decided to move to a better address, knowing that such things are important in American business.

Soon Carlos and I were settled into a two-bedroom apartment on Fifth Avenue, and I regained some of the confidence I felt when I first came to America. My social life began to expand again, and before long I was being invited to dinner parties and other functions.

I told no one about my immigration problems. Certainly none of the people I knew dreamed they were associating with a fugitive from American justice!

At one of the parties I attended I met a brilliant scientist of European birth; a highly intelligent man who held an important position in a major corporation. As I soon learned, he fell in love with me at first sight.

He was solicitous as no American had been, and his mind was so complex that everything he discussed was fascinating. He knew how to pay court to me in a grand style which is common to Europeans, and his sympathy soothed me.

I saw Jan frequently, and one evening, after learning he had become an American citizen, I told him in confidence about my immigration problems. He understood, being European, and recommended a lawyer in Washington who, he said, could solve my problems.

As I saw more of Jan I came to like his savoir faire, and I enjoyed his quiet mockery of New World values. He made me feel less like an alien. His ever-changing ideas enthralled me, and I was flattered by his undeviating interest in every aspect of my life.

What I liked best about our relationship was my freedom to be myself. When I dated an American I had to conceal my intelligence and pretend to be slightly stupid. When I was with Jan the contrary was true. He demanded intellectual honesty, and if I evaded him in a discussion he prodded me into an expression of truth.

Jan was twenty-four years older than I, infinitely more experienced, and I gradually succumbed to his many charms, which for me did not exclude his fine mind. I can't pretend I fell in love with him, but he put me at ease, and I sometimes felt kittenish in his presence. He played the role of a caring father, giving me the attention and love that had been so lacking in my relations with my own father.

Jan carried on a concentrated campaign for five months, and at last I gave in. We were married almost immediately. In spite of the differences in our age he was a vigorous, assured lover, and he swore we would be happy together.

Almost immediately after our marriage Jan endorsed my petition to become a permanent resident of the United States. My friend in Washington went to work again on my behalf, his father and another Senator sponsoring a bill that granted me the right to stay in America. To my astonishment and joy the bill was passed by Congress, which was quite an accomplishment as my very presence in the country had been illegal. After an appropriate period as a resident alien, I could apply for American citizenship.

I continued to work, of course, but soon discovered that my new husband had the European attitude toward women in business. Jan was convinced that no man and woman could enjoy a strictly business relationship, and when I met someone for a business lunch he felt certain the man had other motives in mind. In vain I protested that I had been looking after myself for years and had encountered no problems. Jan forbade me to meet any man for lunch, and it dawned on me that my older husband was afflicted with the curse of jealousy.

We had never discussed my future career before our marriage as I had naïvely assumed I would continue to work. To my chagrin—and distaste—Jan demanded I give up my career. He had expanded his own business interests and earned a very substantial income as a consultant to several large companies. So, he argued, he earned ample money to support Carlos and me in comfort.

When Jan applied pressure, trying to force me to give up my caeer, we quarreled. My business was successful, I had worked very hard to promote it and I saw no reason to abandon it.

I realized the marriage had been a mistake, as grave an error as my first marriage to Juan, and I was tempted to leave Jan. But he had signed my immigration papers and threatened to rescind his support if I left him. I was compelled to stay.

Jan launched a new campaign to force me to submit to his will, and he so overwhelmed me in his efforts to dominate me that I sometimes feared I would lose my identity. In a typical maneuver he would forbid me to talk when we would spend an evening with some of his friends. Then, when I tried to comply with his wishes, he patronized me by telling his friends—in my presence—that while I was obviously beautiful, I was also shy and naïve, unable to join in conversations because of my limited intellectual background. This infuriated me to the point that I deliberately tried to turn the talk into complex philosophical and metaphysical channels. This gave Jan fresh opportunities, and he delighted in twisting my remarks and mocking me so he could prove to his friends that the poor little dear was floundering.

His attempts to dominate me were unsuccessful. I knew, no matter what he said or did, that I was neither naïve nor stupid, and I had no intention of permitting him to grind me down. I did realize that he was a man with inner problems of which I had been unaware before I had married him. I had no idea why he found it necessary to humiliate me, to build himself up at my expense, but I refused to gratify his ego at the expense of my own identity.

He regarded my business as a direct challenge, and it became increasingly difficult for me to function. Jan made his office in our apartment, and he seemed to spend as much time spying on me as he did attending to his own business. He objected when I wrote business letters or worked on my accounts. He went into a rage whenever I spoke to my partner on the telephone, and finally he issued an ultimatum forbidding me to have any such conversations. In order to talk to my partner I had to dream up excuses to leave the apartment and make my calls from a public telephone.

Jan came home late one Friday afternoon, several months after he began his assault of my business acumen. He looked at me with a tight smile. "I've accepted a permanent job with a company in Houston, Texas," he said, "and we're leaving tomorrow afternoon in a station wagon I've rented. And I've already placed an ad in the newspapers to sublet this apartment."

I lost my temper and we had a wild argument, but Jan refused to budge. Our plans were made, and nothing would persuade him to change them or listen to reason.

I can best reveal my state of mind by quoting an entry I made that night in my diary:

This evening Jan came home with the devastating order for us to leave New York. It is midnight, and I cannot sleep. Jan is sound asleep, and I have to watch out for the creaking of the doors as I come to my desk to write.

I see my life like a house with many doors and windows open. Jan has closed them all for me and I am trapped inside. I am responsible for what is happening, even in this impasse. I should not think I cannot change my destiny. I must break the link with the past and my background and my country. I must become a permanent resident once and for all and have my legal status finalized. I must gather my strength and go with this monster to Texas. I can't give him the opportunity to withdraw his signature on my papers. I'm being victimized. He's a blackmailer. I know that from his cunning eyes. I distrust him, but he's not going to break my spirit, regardless of how intelligent he is. My projects, my ideas will remain clear in my mind, no matter how he pollutes my being.

We are at war, and I will win. I can wait. Even if my business suffers, I'll start another. When will we women really be free? I wait for the day when we are not victimized by decisions, resolutions, transfers imposed upon us by men. I hope I live to see that day. In America changes come rapidly.

If things become too difficult in the months ahead I will retreat into my fantasies, my dreams, my secret places of the spirit. My dreams today have a symbolic shape. Someday they will be reality. I'll be independent and have a place among the Americans. Little by little I feel room is being made for me, complete room . . ."

I made a bed for Carlos in the station wagon and packed as many of our belongings as we could carry. We were leaving in such a hurry, however, that I had to make arrangements with a moving company to follow us into the apartment on Monday and ship most of our belongings to us as soon as we had a permanent address.

The trip to Houston was a nightmare. My husband had tried amateur racing in Monaco, and drove like a madman. One day he drove on the wrong side of a two-lane highway, and was able to avoid hitting an oncoming car only by climbing onto the embankment. I was a nervous wreck by the time we reached Houston.

We found a motel on the outskirts of Houston and moved into two rooms. Jan immediately went off to his office, taking the station wagon, and I was stranded, miles from shopping centers and even farther from the downtown district.

For days I did nothing but continue the reading lessons I was giving Carlos. I was so miserable I wept frequently, and my son wiped away my tears with his little hands. He was and is marvelously sensitive, and without him the task ahead of me would have been almost impossible to accomplish. I say "almost" because, even without him, I would not have allowed myself to be crushed.

After several days I forced myself to organize. Jan had a three-year contract, so I would find a house, then search for ways to keep myself occupied. I told myself that any problem could be solved. I was not going to feel sorry for myself any longer, and I would not permit my situation to destroy me. Carlos needed me, and the only person I had to depend on was myself. So depend on myself I would.

When I told Jan I wanted to find a house he immediately believed I had given in to him, and I let him think what he pleased. It would be far easier for me to rebuild my life if I didn't have to fight him every step of the way.

The women I met in various real estate offices were helpful—and talkative. I had never lived anywhere in the United States except New York, so I had much to learn about local customs and conditions in Houston. In the back of my mind was the determination to start a new business of some kind so I could become totally independent of Jan, and I knew enough about America to realize that a different approach to business is required in various parts of the country. The New York pace was frenzied; Houston was slower and more social. Key decisions were often made over lunch or cocktails, with lots of idle chatter thrown in as filler.

I found a lovely old house with a large lawn, and after our furniture from New York had been installed, I began to feel more secure. I needed mobility, so I withdrew some money from my New York savings account and bought a small car with good mileage. Then I was ready.

First, I visited city authorities to learn what products were made in Houston, what had to be brought in from the outside and what potentials existed for new industries. I felt at home dealing with industrial products, thanks to my background, and I steered myself in that direction.

I soon realized petrochemicals were not for me, the various companies were already well organized and staffed. I visited a number of electronics corporations, and had several long talks with high-ranking officials who were marvelously hospitable. In New York I would have needed introductions to these executives, but in Houston my desire to learn was all I needed to win a cordial welcome.

Again I found a well-organized industry where there was no need for my services. Also, I recognized my limitations. I lacked the technical education necessary to make a place for myself in electronics. I was perplexed, not knowing what direction to take.

While I was still searching for a future, my son was hospitalized with a bad throat infection, and during the two weeks of his stay I spent most of my time with him. Soon I found myself developing an interest in the hospital boom that was taking place in Houston, and after questioning the doctors and nurses with whom I came in contact I began to visit the administrators of several hospitals.

It didn't take me long to grasp the fundamentals, and I soon found out how hospitals functioned, what businesses were essential to their operations and what facilities already existed to supply them. Knowing that hospital building in Houston was mushrooming, and with the city developing into a major medical center, I became convinced there was a future for me in hospital supplies.

Before doing anything else I made a thorough study of the business. I spent a great deal of time at the Houston hospitals, I read everything I could find and I opened a correspondence with major manufacturers in St. Louis, New York and Connecticut.

I had twenty-five thousand dollars in cash and kept eight thousand aside for use only in emergencies. That left me seventeen thousand dollars to start my business. I formed a corporation, but knew I had to visit the manufacturers before I could open an office.

Jan was opposed to the idea of my making trips, and refused to allow me to leave Houston.

Fortunately, Jan's employers sent him off to Argentina on a business trip that would force him to spend a considerable period of time in South America. His absence gave me the freedom to do what I pleased.

I rented a small office within walking distance of our house. This would make it possible for me to come home at noon every day to have lunch with Carlos.

Then I went to a department store and bought a

beautiful wardrobe, which included a very French hat. At last I was ready, and went off on my trip. Because I was a married woman I was treated with respect, but I soon learned the manufacturers were satisfied with the Houston dealer to whom they had granted franchises. I was able to persuade them to grant me six franchises, two of them important, when I volunteered to make my peace with the Houston dealer.

When I returned home I was thrilled to discover that several other manufacturers to whom I had written also were willing to sell me merchandise. Then I called the local dealer, who was amused by my accent and agreed to see me.

I dressed as an ingenue, kept my makeup to a minimum, and put a band in my hair. I looked sixteen instead of twenty-six, and I bubbled with girlish enthusiasm, telling him what fun it would be to operate my very own business.

He reacted as I had hoped. I'd be no competition, and after warning me that hospital administrators would make passes at me, he promised to write to some of the major manufacturers recommending me and saying he had no objection if they wanted to give me franchises for several of their products.

I ordered a small supply of thermometers, syringes, gauzes and bandages. I visited every hospital, and going through the yellow pages of the telephone book, I systematically called on every physician who was listed. Leaving my business card, I promised twenty-four-hour delivery, stressing that I specialized in personal service. I made it clear that the one thing I couldn't do was to extend long-term credit, and most of the doctors I saw were sympathetic, agreeing to pay within eight days.

In my enthusiasm I expanded too rapidly. I spent almost all of the ten thousand dollars I had budgeted for supplies, but I had as yet received very few cash orders in return. I desperately needed credit, and decided to go straight to the vice president of the bank at which I had opened my account.

I knew I had a tough job on my hands as I sat across the huge desk of that giant Texan. He was courtly in an old-fashioned way, and his attitude was unyielding. Without collateral he couldn't grant me a line of credit. My "French" accent was charming, but it wouldn't get me very far in Houston, a city that still had a frontier mentality.

As he lectured me his interest in my legs became increasingly obvious.

Finally I decided to attack. "I intend to accomplish nothing with my legs and body," I said. "In business I use my mind."

I had caught him, and he was embarrassed.

Pushing my seeming advantage, I asked for a modest five thousand dollars, saying that after I repaid it within a month I would like it expanded to fifteen thousand.

Again he refused, saying he would loan me nothing without collateral.

I demanded that he write down his reasons for his lack of faith in me. I wanted the souvenir.

Again he refused.

I had shown him all the documents pertaining to my business, and I lost my temper. If I were a man, I told him, he would have granted me the loan, so I had to assume the bank had a secret slogan: "For Men Only."

Then I threatened to go to all of the bank's prominent women customers and persuade them to withdraw their accounts.

I wasn't bluffing, and the banker knew it. Rather than be forced to tolerate the fuss I intended to make he gave in, and granted me the loan, but on very stiff terms.

I accepted, still resenting him but looking forward to the challenge. A woman had to be more efficient than a man, I realized, if she wanted to succeed in business.

At this critical time in my professional life my husband returned from Argentina, and the temporary peace Carlos and I had enjoyed was shattered. I couldn't keep my business life a secret from Jan, so I told him about it, openly defying him, even though my permanent immigration permit hadn't yet materialized. I was relying on the hope that, as he was new to Houston, he wouldn't want to create a scandal that might jeopardize his own position.

My tactics succeeded, but at the same time they backfired. My greatest weakness was my love for my son, and my husband knew it, so he deliberately became abusive and nasty to the little boy. I had to arrange my schedule so I would return home each day before Jan arrived from his office. And when I had to make deliveries to doctors late in the day I always took Carlos with me. Under no circumstances would I allow him to be alone with Jan.

It was unnecessary for me to explain the situation to Carlos, who understood. Sometimes, especially when Jan shouted and made scenes, my son and I exchanged quick glances and achieved a complete rapport. We grew closer than ever, but I was worried because he was so thin. I resorted to all kinds of little tricks to persuade him to eat, and this so infuriated Jan that he became violent, smashing our best dishes on the floor.

It was obvious to me that I had to leave him as soon as I could, but in the meantime there were complications. He demanded his marital rights, so I allowed him to make love to me rather than let an unpleasant situation become worse. It was plain that my income from the doctors wasn't enough for me to support myself, so I paid more visits to the city's hospitals, hounding the administrators and purchasing agents.

I felt ill when the Immigration and Naturalization Service returned my application. Jan had failed to fill out every question on the form, so there would be another delay of at least six months before my new status would be granted. That meant I had to tolerate an additional six months of hell.

Thanks to my efforts at the hospitals my orders increased, but it was their practice to pay for merchandise either thirty or sixty days after delivery, and I was afraid to ask them to make an exception for me. Aware that a new crisis was brewing, I decided to meet it before it erupted. Wearing my best dress and dabbing French perfume behind my ears, I returned to the office of the bank vice president.

First I repaid the initial loan in full, and then asked for a much larger credit line, thirty-three thousand dollars, which I needed to fill a major hospital order. I could produce only a letter of intent, not a formal order, so my request was turned down.

I stalked out and drove straight to another bank, calming myself before I faced the head of the branch office. I used charm to sell myself, but I was totally honest with him, which impressed him, and he realized I knew my business. The next day the loan was granted, on condition that I not try to obtain credit from any other bank.

I made my delivery of merchandise on schedule, and then received an order from a hospital under construction in Dallas. After being in business for five months I had turned the corner, and my operation was profitable.

I hired a salesman who would deliver as well as sell supplies, and after dinner every night I packed the merchandise he would take to our customers the next day. One night when I went to our small warehouse to check the inventory, I caught the salesman stealing a few syringes and other goods. I agreed not to prosecute him in return for repayment, but I had to discharge him, and again was shorthanded.

I hired a maid to take care of the house, believing I could use my own time to better advantage if someone else did the cleaning. So I was relieved of that pressure.

Other pressures became overwhelming. My husband was bored by his job and resigned in order to spend his whole time developing a grandiose idea, the establishment of a telecommunications network in South America. His plan was brilliant but impractical, partly because it was so expensive and in part because its realization would have required the cooperation of every South American government. I knew enough about South America to realize the political obstacles could not be overcome. I told Jan the truth when he asked my advice, and my honesty infuriated him. That was too bad, but I knew his scheme wouldn't work out.

He worked at home, which created new complications for me. The presence of the maid every morning inhibited him from harassing Carlos, and I was able to make arrangements with sympathetic neighbors, who took care of my son in the afternoons before I returned home. At best, however, the arrangement was precarious and makeshift.

One afternoon Carlos had returned home before I arrived, and when I walked in the house I found Jan trying to hold the child's head under water in the kitchen sink. I realized my husband was truly demented, and knowing my physical strength was no match for his, I had to distract him. I seized a large plate and threw it on the floor as hard as I could, smashing it. He released my poor, sputtering Carlos, who managed to escape. Jan stared down at the broken plate and all of his anger drained away.

I thought I would lose my own mind, but the worst was yet to come. A visit to a physician confirmed my fear that I was pregnant.

Six

My troubles continued to multiply. Jan's funds were limited, the cost of establishing his telecommunications network was enormous, and overnight his opposition to my career vanished. He was earning no money, so the profits from my hospital supply business provided our only income.

My business was prospering at last, fortunately, and I was again able to hire a salesman. But my opportunities for further expansion were cut off when Jan demanded a loan of ten thousand dollars. When I balked, he became ugly and threatened to withdraw his sponsorship of my permanent residency, saying he would tell the immigration authorities I was unfit to stay in the country.

Much later I would realize it would have been very difficult for him to persuade the government to deport me, but in my ignorance and fright I believed him, and advanced him the money. He went off for an extended stay in the Caribbean, intending to set up his headquarters there, and I felt it was worth the large sum of money to be rid of him. I had lost my security, but had gained a temporary peace of mind.

I celebrated my husband's departure by making a trip to New York, where I attended the theater every night and visited friends. Far more important, I held several meetings with my partner in the used car business. Competition was increasing, limiting our profits, and we agreed to switch from second-hand cars to trucks, which were in great demand. I planned, after the birth of my new baby, to make another tour of South America to visit our clients. By that time, I hoped, my immigration status would be settled.

I was optimistic about the future of my original business when I returned to Houston, and the hospital supply company continued to grow. I repaid the bank loan of thirty-three thousand dollars, and obtained another for seventy thousand, using my receivables as collateral. I hired a second salesman, then a third, and had to call on fewer clients myself. I was able to function as an executive now, and on weekends I could devote my full attention to Carlos. The continuing absence of Jan was a joy.

I began to develop a modest social life for the first time since moving to Texas, and not only accepted a number of invitations but gave several small dinner parties. Through some European friends I met an Austrian heart specialist who was in Houston on an extended visit. He was an exceptionally interesting man, and we had what I have since called my silent romance. If I hadn't been five months pregnant the relationship might not have remained platonic. Even so, because of me he twice delayed his return to Austria.

Once my business was on solid ground I became daring and invited the banker who had rejected my loan request to have lunch with me. He accepted, probably out of curiosity, and I lost no time telling him the progress I had made. Naturally I stressed the helpful cooperation I had received from his competitors.

A short time later I took possession of a larger warehouse. A day or two later the branch manager of the original bank, which was virtually my neighbor, called on me and offered his bank's services unconditionally. When I asked what he meant he suggested I visit the main office.

I did, and my old antagonist now offered me extensive credit. I accepted, feeling I had won a great victory. I also convinced the bank that had given the original loan to let me go elsewhere for the new loan. I told them I wanted to spread the credit risk, and they agreed. I had my private reasons for obtaining additional loans: I had big plans, and was thinking of opening branch offices in Dallas and San Antonio.

New orders poured in, and I hired a secretary, then a clerk. I learned from the salesmen even as I supervised their activities, and in my spare time I kept a card file on every physician and hospital purchasing agent who was a client. Business tripled, supporting five of us in comfort, and I was earning a respectable profit. Every hour counted, and never had I worked so hard.

Shortly before my baby was due I paid another, very quick, visit to New York. My income from my real estate ventures had been declining, so I took the business away from an agent who had been handling it for me and gave it to a friend I had known from my early days in America. The used car business had come to a standstill, and I agreed with my partner that I needed to pay another visit to South America, but I couldn't leave the

United States until my precious immigration permit arrived.

I returned to Houston, and my heart sank when I found that my husband had come home from the Caribbean. He was filled with enthusiasm for his telecommunications network and never stopped smiling, but I knew better than to believe he had improved. The moment he was crossed or disappointed his mood would change.

He urged me to have an injection that would induce premature childbirth so I could accompany him as an interpreter and sales chief when he went to South America. Rather than risk an argument I didn't even point out to him that I couldn't leave the United States until I received the papers making me a permanent resident.

I refused to allow the approach of my new baby to interfere with my work. In the final weeks of my pregnancy I suffered from insomnia, so I worked on plans to expand the business, and intended to visit San Antonio and Corpus Christi as soon as possible after I gave birth.

A few hours before I went off to the hospital I paid a business visit to my old enemy-friend, the bank vice president, and he was so nervous he agreed without a murmur to my loan requests. Before I left his office he begged me not to return when I was in such an advanced state of pregnancy because, he said, "I don't want problems here."

That same day I raced to the hospital, where I gave birth to my second son, whom I named Arnim.

The knowledge that Jan was at home with Carlos made me so apprehensive that only two days after

Arnim was born I persuaded the hospital to let me take my new baby home. Less than a week later I returned to work.

In February, 1960, two months after Arnim was born, I finally received my "green card" from the United States government. That card was the key to my freedom, giving me a status I had lacked for six years. I was proud to be a permanent resident of the United States, and I felt that at last America wanted me. How wonderful it felt to be wanted!

By this time I was supporting my husband, and his future plans depended on my goodwill and cooperation. He was consistently pleasant, and so docile I sometimes felt ill.

He pestered me incessantly, urging me to go to South America with him. As it happened, his plans coincided with my own desires, and as I knew the presence of a male escort would save me complications and embarrassments, I consented.

I had one practical problem. The green card guaranteed my reentry into the United States, but another five years would pass before I could obtain American citizenship, therefore I had no passport in which to put the visas I needed for several countries.

I solved the problem in my own way. I took the covers of an old, passport-sized book and made it into a document of my own. On the first page I typed, THIS IS NOT A PASSPORT. On the second page was an affadavit containing the place and date of my birth, my vital statistics and a photograph, which I signed and had sealed by a notary public. The remaining pages were blank, and the consulates of the various South American countries obligingly filled them with the visas I would need.

A Houston lawyer who had handled my legal work agreed to supervise the operations of my hospital supply business during my absence.

It also occured to me that I might be able to expand the second-hand car company into a much larger export-import business in due time. I spent a day at the Rice University library, making a study of the natural resources and raw materials of the various countries I intended to visit. I had no specific ideas about new business ventures, but I had learned that small business depends upon individual performance. It would be up to me to devise some way to coordinate the hospital supply business with any new projects I might develop.

I made arrangements with someone who was very competent to take care of the children.

Another problem was the financing of the trip. I had no intention of paying for my husband's considerable travel expenses out of my pocket, so I wrote to various people I knew in New York, asking if they wanted to hire us as consultants on our trip. I received two replies, one to make an economic survey of Peru and the other to obtain seismic studies of Bolivia and Chile. That took care of expenses.

I prepared the way by writing at length to the governments of Brazil, Uruguay, Argentina, Chile, Peru, Bolivia and Colombia. The scheme for the establishment of the telecommunications network was presented in such glowing terms not one government representative could hide his interest.

As a result, my husband and I were flown everywhere in government aircraft. Receptions, lunches and dinners were given in our honor, and our photographs appeared in leading newspapers everywhere. In between social occasions I obtained large quantities of data for our consultant studies.

The trip, which lasted forty days, was a brilliant social success. Business result: zero.

Something else, totally unexpected, developed during that trip. For the first time since our marriage Jan and I did not quarrel, and our relations were as pleasant as they had been during our courtship. He was spending every hour of the day and night with me, so he had no cause to become upset, and as Carlos was back home in Houston there was no reason for him to be jealous. His mind still fascinated me when he was functioning at his best, and although I could have left him now, thanks to my permanent resident status, I decided to give our marriage another chance. My financial independence and my new security relieved many pressures, enabling me to become more generous.

Jan taught me how to prepare reports, and when we returned home we went into business together, forming a company we called Telecommunications Management Consultants. Jan was such a profound, advanced thinker that there were few business opportunities for him in Houston, and this new company might have enabled him to use his extraordinary talents.

Every night, after dinner, we worked together preparing letters to large companies, offering them our services. Jan's expertise was the basic ingredient, and we were hired as consultants by one of the large Detroit motorcar manufacturers and by a major engineering firm in New York. These jobs made it possible for Jan to pay a share of our living expenses and because he was less dependent upon me our relations improved still more.

In addition I arranged for Carlos, who was now six years old, to engage in various activities of instruction—supervised play and the like—away from home during the day. This eliminated the friction between him and my husband for most of our waking hours. I must admit my apprehensions weren't completely dispelled, but I learned to live from day to day, and had no cause for complaint.

I was the business partner of the team, and had to make fairly frequent trips to visit our clients in Detroit and New York for a day or two at a time. These separations were good for me and equally good for Jan, further easing the tensions between us. In fact, I was no longer afraid of leaving him in the house with Carlos, although I must admit that the presence of servants as buffers contributed to my new peace of mind.

I was so busy I had little time to think about myself, so my romanticism was held in check. My relationship, such as it was, with the Austrian cardiologist, soon died a natural death.

Occasionally, particularly on Sundays, I felt life had cheated me. I was successful in business, ambitious to do still better, and money was no longer a problem. I had two wonderful children, and gave them all of my affection. But something was missing.

That something was the love of a strong man, someone closer to my own age than Jan, who would give me the recognition I still craved. I couldn't pretend to myself that I loved Jan. I was still in awe of the depths of his scientific mind, but his temperament was so mercurial that I had to cater to him constantly, soothing him and bolstering his ego. Often he inched toward a new explosion that would ruin everything, but at the last moment backed away.

Certainly he paid scant attention to my own needs. He listened to me only when we discussed our mutual work, and the rest of the time my words dropped into a void. Naturally he displayed no interest in the operations of my other businesses, and he paid no attention to the running of the household.

I might have forgiven him everything had he not been so indifferent to the children. His hostility toward Carlos was controlled, but still lurked close to the surface, and he was beginning to regard Arnim—his own son—as a rival, too.

Our sex life, such as it was, gave me no satisfaction, perhaps because Jan sought only his own pleasure. My erotic dreams were vivid, and I scolded myself, saying that what I wanted was an adventurous lover, a philosopher, someone strong, gentle and successful, all wrapped up in one handsome, charming man. I told myself I was being a sentimental adolescent, and should be contented with what I had achieved.

But my dreams continued to nag at me, and I became obsessive in my approach to my work. I visited so many hospitals and nursing homes that only my card-file system enabled me to differentiate between the people I met. I worked with Jan on our consultant business. I kept an eye on my real estate properties. I planned new ventures after I went to bed at night, then changed them the next day. I realized that what I was doing wasn't healthy, that I was escaping into my work, but at the same time I knew I was building my defenses for the day when the inevitable storm broke.

Jan went off to Detroit on a business trip, returning unexpectedly one night. He burst into my bedroom, shouting incoherently, and I gathered he had quarreled with a motor company executive, which meant our contract would not be renewed.

He came closer to me, and although the room was cool I could see the beads of perspiration at his hairline. He grabbed my shoulders, and I was terrified.

Suddenly he was shouting something about airplanes on fire, and I knew he was talking about his wartime experiences. He had been a brave pilot, decorated many times in World War II, but until this moment he had concealed the horrible memories that poured out of him.

I did what I could to soothe him, conquering my own terror, and at last he sank into a chair. Then the words erupted from him. First he revealed that for years he had suffered from blinding headaches, never finding relief from them and never mentioning them to anyone because he had been afraid he was going mad.

He hated the whole world, and cursed until he was breathless.

He put his hands over his face, weeping and sobbing until I thought his chest would burst. The scene lasted all night.

The next day I wrote a few lines hurriedly in my diary: "The giant became human. He cried. He exposed his neuroticism. He, the brave, decorated soldier, exposed his terror and fear for life in general. Eroticism, travels and love will pass him by. His stiffness wavered and thus the powerful Jan was completely destroyed and he sank."

It was obvious to me that Jan was desperately in need of the psychiatric help he had avoided for so long. I made the mistake of suggesting that he seek help, and named a doctor he should see.

Jan's mood changed instantly, and his rage was directed a me. He cursed and ranted, picking up bric-a-brac, bottles of perfume—everything he could snatch from my dressing table—and smashing them on the floor. His eyes gleamed, and I could see he was enjoying the destruction for its own sake.

I was terrified.

He accused me of leading him on, teasing him, playing with his emotions. Threatening to beat me and shouting that I deserved it, he stormed out of the room.

The children were my first concern, and I dashed out another door, brought them into the bedroom with me and locked us in. Then I called a physician, and as soon as I explained the situation to him he said he would come to the house immediately.

He did, but at first Jan refused to see him. The doctor knew how to handle people in this predicament, and finally calmed Jan enough to persuade him to take a tranquilizing shot. He fell into a deep sleep and the doctor left after telling me to persuade my husband to seek psychiatric help without delay.

Carlos went off to school, and I took Arnim, his bottle and a crib to the office with me. I didn't dare leave him alone in the house with his father.

When I returned at noon Jan was awake, rational and busily engaged in designing an electronic desk. He greeted me affectionately, asked where the children had gone and obviously remembered nothing of his night-long episode.

I launched my campaign, urging him to see a psychiatrist.

He looked at me in honest bewilderment. "But why should I?" he asked, and then closed the subject with a gentle but firm, "There's nothing wrong with me."

That was the beginning of a time of terror unlike any other I have ever known. I lived in constant dread, afraid my children and I would be killed when Jan suffered another of his spells. I couldn't have him committed to an institution because he was quite in full possession of his faculties and treated all of us with consideration. Yet I never knew when the next outbreak might occur.

Always afraid I might trigger a violent response, I continued to press for a psychiatrist. Jan invariably replied that he had never been healthier.

I took yet another approach, suggesting an amicable separation. If he encountered difficulties earning a living, I told him, I would gladly share my income with him.

He invariably refused, saying he couldn't live without me and the boys. Then he apologized for his "bad temper," and calmly dismissed the whole matter from his mind.

His affection for Arnim was real, so I rationalized that my younger son was relatively safe. But I was desperately afraid for Carlos. The child was aware of the tensions and became expert in avoiding subjects that might push his stepfather over the brink again. But the poor child paid a heavy penalty for his discretion, and often late at night, when I couldn't sleep, I could hear that he too was awake, playing with his toys in the adjoining bedroom.

Obviously something needed to be done to end the frightful impasse before someone was badly injured or murdered.

Seven

My life became still more complicated when Jan, who had nothing better to occupy his time, worked up the same petty jealousy that he'd shown in the early days of our marriage. He called me at my office several times each day, and if I happened to be visiting a client he would telephone all over town until he found me. Then he would berate and threaten the man whose office I was visiting. This scandalous behavior caused a great deal of talk, and it was plain to me that my business soon would suffer.

I called a lawyer whom both of us knew socially, hoping he could talk Jan into a separation. My husband refused to visit the attorney's office, calling instead one of my most important clients and telling him lies about me. Jan said he would use these same tactics every time I as much as mentioned a separation.

I decided to try another approach. If Jan could be persuaded to take a job in some other city we would be separated, for all practical purposes. He had been claiming he was too old to be hired by anyone, but I began a subtle campaign of building up his ego again. Swallowing my loathing for this sick monster who was making our lives unbearable, I went out for a walk with him after dinner every evening, suffering the humid night air of Houston as I tried to persuade him he had valuable contributions to make to industry.

At last he became sufficiently convinced to write letters to various corporations. His reputation was greater than he knew, and he had a number of interesting responses. Among them was the offer of a position with a major corporation in Wichita, Kansas, and he accepted it. He went off at once, establishing a routine of staying in Wichita through the workweek and spending a large chunk of his salary on airplane tickets so he could fly home weekends.

This situation was far from perfect, but at least it was an improvement. I was able to think about business again, and not only worked to repair the damage Jan had done but began a campaign to get new accounts.

I soon discovered I could no longer lose myself in my work. I was merely evading my basic problem instead of facing it, and I realized I would know no peace of mind until I found a lasting solution.

Some days I was overwhelmed by my dilemma, but my primitive instinct for self-preservation proved stronger than my fears. Somehow I would overcome my problem and achieve both security and peace for my children and myself. Like Scarlett O'Hara, I refused to admit defeat.

One morning I decided to take the day off from work, something I had never done, and drove to the Galveston beach with my sons. There, I swore to the children that our lives would take a sharp turn for the better and that

I would not let them lead a mediocre life, that I would make them proud of me and that finally the three of us would be liberated and happy.

Arnim was too small to grasp what I was saying, but Carlos understood and grinned at me. "Okay, Mummy," he said.

Okay, Mummy! We had made a solemn pact. I intended to keep it. The next time I faced a crisis in my relations with Jan, as I was sure I would, I would stop procrastinating.

My inner stand renewed my energies, and in the next few weeks I added a new company to my growing business, going into partnership with the owner of a hospital supply company in San Antonio. His system of providing warehouse space for merchandise was marvelously efficient; he worked as hard as I did, and the improvement in my vocational situation cheered me.

Then one day, suddenly, Jan came and announced he had resigned. He had invented a device that was a failure, he said, so he quit before the company realized it had wasted a large sum of money on something that was useless.

All of my old fears encompassed me again.

A day or two later, while Jan was out of the house, his employer in Wichita telephoned him, and in his absence spoke at length to me. He told me Jan had one of the most brilliant minds he had ever known and that he had tried at length to dissuade him from resigning. He was calling in the forlorn hope that he could persuade my husband to return.

When I repeated the conversation to Jan he stuck to his story, refusing to believe his position was still open for him. Under no circumstances would he return the telephone call.

Each morning I left him sunbathing as I went off to my office, and I knew I was drifting back into the mess that had eased for a time. I was startled by the realization that Jan demanded failure, that he wouldn't be truly satisfied until he destroyed himself. This was the root of his trouble, and I was allowing myself and my children to be influenced by it.

At that moment I decided to give him an ultimatum: Either he would undertake psychiatric counseling without delay or I would start divorce proceedings.

As a first step I visited a psychiatrist, hoping to prepare the ground for Jan's treatment. The doctor told me that when a patient is deeply depressed the family must be tolerant and understanding. He also stressed that if I threw Jan out of the house he might do serious harm to himself.

So much for my ultimatum. Could I be less than compassionate? Did I have the right to force a sick man to injure himself?

For the moment I temporized, trying to find a clear line of action. Jan, who had nothing better to do, began to make abusive telephone calls to the hospital administrators, purchasing agents and physicians who were my clients. Houston may be a large city, but it has a small town atmosphere, and I realized that soon my business reputation would be seriously compromised.

Unable to procrastinate any longer, I decided to take a major step. I would sell my business while I could still command a good price for it. I would return to New York, and eventually would invest my substantial profit in other enterprises. First, however, I would take positive steps to end my personal crisis.

I sold the business, had my household belongings shipped east, and taking the children with me, I returned to New York. Jan stayed behind in Houston to attend to the disposal of our house.

The boys and I arrived in New York on a hot day in July, 1961. I rented an apartment on the upper East Side, my favorite part of town, and made an immediate appointment with an attorney I knew and trusted. I poured out my whole story to him.

He was not encouraging. I could not lock my husband out of our apartment. I could not force Jan to accept either psychiatric treatment as an outpatient or admission to a mental hospital. And I could not obtain a divorce from him on grounds of mental deterioration.

The lawyer offered me only one ray of hope. If Jan joined the children and me and became violent, I should call the police to restrain him. Then, but only then could I obtain a court order forbidding him to enter the premises.

I was incredulous. "You mean," I demanded, "that I have to wait until he assaults thc children or me before I can have him locked out?"

"That's the law," my attorney said.

As I returned to our new apartment from his office I hated New York. I hated the United States. I hated all laws. Most of all, I hated men.

The fear that Jan would arrive at any time obsessed me. In my mind he became even more vicious and unpredictable than he had been in real life. I dreamed about him at night and would wake up in a cold sweat.

Each day's freedom might be my last. I thought of vanishing, going off to Europe with the boys and leaving no forwarding address. Only the knowledge that my funds wouldn't last forever held me back.

One day I took the children to Jones Beach, and again the sand and sea comforted me. I realized I had to rid myself of the paralysis that was gripping me, and that only by becoming active again could I reorder my life. I needed an income, and the sooner I went to work the better off I'd be. When and if Jan reappeared I would face the crisis, but until then I couldn't spend my days doing nothing.

After we came home from the beach I gave the children their dinner, put them to bed and then put myself through the process of comparative analysis in which I hadn't engaged for several years. I knew that many occupations would be open to me if I invested the profits I had made from my hospital supply business, but I had no idea how much I might need if and when Jan appeared, so I decided to keep that money in ready cash. Therefore I would look for a position that paid a salary.

A process of elimination led me to decide that an advertising agency might be right, particularly one with enough foreign business to utilize my knowledge of languages. I had been dealing with the top people in many companies, so I might qualify as an account executive. I believed I had an ability to express my thoughts on paper, so I wouldn't be out of line if I looked for a place as a copywriter.

I prepared a summary of my vocational background and submitted it to a number of agencies. Several interviewed me, but stressed that there were no openings on an appropriate level; if I came in on a lower scale, they said, I would find the work frustrating.

I decided to take a different approach and apply for any job that might be available. Soon I was interviewed for a post as a secretary with bilingual skills. I was a fairly efficient typist, but I had no knowledge of shorthand, and I was surprised when I was hired.

There I was, perched on a stiff revolving chair, writing letters—again and again. My boss was very fussy about punctuation and form, so I had to type some letters as many as four times before he was satisfied. At the end of a week I decided the agony wasn't worth his time or mine, so I offered him my resignation. He refused to accept it, saying I was more than proving my worth because of what I knew about business conditions in South America.

This was precisely the opening I had wanted, so I was happy to stay, and I began to snoop. Whenever my boss went out of town, attended meetings or was otherwise occupied, I went from department to department, talking to people, asking questions. I read reports, I studied files, I looked at correspondence. I arrived early at the office, and I stayed late. I took piles of documents home with me, read them after dinner and returned them the next morning.

There is no substitute for thoroughness and application to detail. I learned from junior executives and from the secretaries of senior executives, from anyone and everyone who could and would contribute to my knowledge of the company's affairs. It is surprising how much information can be gleaned about an operation in a relatively short time.

As I studied the advertising agency's affairs, certain strengths and weaknesses began to become clear to me. It was the weaknesses that interested me, especially those with Latin America, and I concentrated on them in depth. Ultimately I realized I could perform a valuable function, but no such job existed, which meant I would have to create it for myself.

I waited until an appropriate time and then, one evening after most of the staff had gone home, I went to the office of a senior executive. He asked what he could do for me, and I told him the question was what I could do for him. Naturally he looked at me with great suspicion.

I pointed out that the agency was in danger of losing an account with a drug house that did considerable South American business, as well as with an airline that had South American routes. I suggested the use of certain tactics to improve the relationship, and before our talk ended he offered me a new job as something of an assistant account executive doing liaison work.

I started as soon as my old boss was able to hire a new secretary, and soon was spending a great deal of time with members of the advertising departments of the drug company and the airline. Most of the problems that had plagued relations with the agency were caused by a lack of knowledge of Latin ways, and I made a number of simple suggestions that smoothed paths.

My new job was almost too easy, and my ambition began to nag me, so I asked for permission to write copy in Spanish for use in South America, in addition to my other duties. The company brass was delighted. So I had more duties and another raise in salary.

But my ambitions backfired on me. Copywriting requires quiet for concentration, and my desk was located in a noisy bullpen where typewriters were clacking, secretaries were talking and file clerks were pausing to gossip. I went to the personnel manager, asking for a corner of my own somewhere, but he replied that space was at a premium and he couldn't do anything for me. After three such requests were turned down, it dawned on me that he didn't like me.

One day I stumbled onto a small storage room filled with nothing but old files piled in boxes. The next time the personnel manager came through the bullpen I halted him, told him to listen to the noise and asked for the use of the storage room.

He said he took complaints only in his office.

I reminded him I had gone to his office three times.

He shrugged and turned me down again.

I exploded. Picking up every heavy book I could find, I threw them, one by one, onto the floor at his feet. I told him what I thought of him, shouted, "I quit!" and stormed out.

The following morning two of the agency's top executives made a joint call to me and asked me to return. I agreed, provided I was given a substantial increase in salary, a new status and an office of my own, no matter how small. All three requests were granted, and I went back to work the following morning. I had come a long way in three months at the agency and felt I had cause to be proud of myself.

One evening, late in autumn—about four weeks after my "coup" at the ad agency—I heard a commotion in the apartment as I emerged from the elevator on our floor. There was a jumble of voices, but the one that cut through all the others was Carlos' voice. He was crying hysterically.

I was so nervous I rang the bell instead of using my key, and a badly upset baby-sitter came to the door. I pushed into the living room; my worst fears were confirmed, there was Jan.

I told him our life together was ended, that I planned to divorce him, and I asked him to leave. I had dreaded this moment, but I was very calm on the surface.

Jan refused to go, and began to argue with me.

I went straight to the house telephone and summoned the doorman of the apartment house.

Leaving the doorman to squabble with Jan, I took the children and went to the apartment of a neighbor. There I telephoned my lawyer, who was on the verge of leaving his office for the day.

He told me he would deal with Jan and instructed me not to return to the apartment until he came for me.

A short time later the lawyer arrived and confronted Jan. I still don't know precisely what was said, but the lawyer managed to convince my husband that I was serious in my intention to obtain a divorce. Under no circumstances would I live under the same roof with him.

Jan left, and I returned to my apartment with the children.

The next day my lawyer drew up my divorce application. Our nightmare had come to an end, or so I thought, but the last act of the drama had yet to be played.

The building staff was under strict orders not to admit Jan to the apartment house, and as I had never

With my nurse in 1935.

At eight years old.

My wedding day, May 3, 1952. My father is next to Juan.

A country afternoon outing for Carlos and me.

This portrait was taken between my first and second marriages.

With Jan (left), as we were about to embark on our South American "consulting" trip. April 1960.

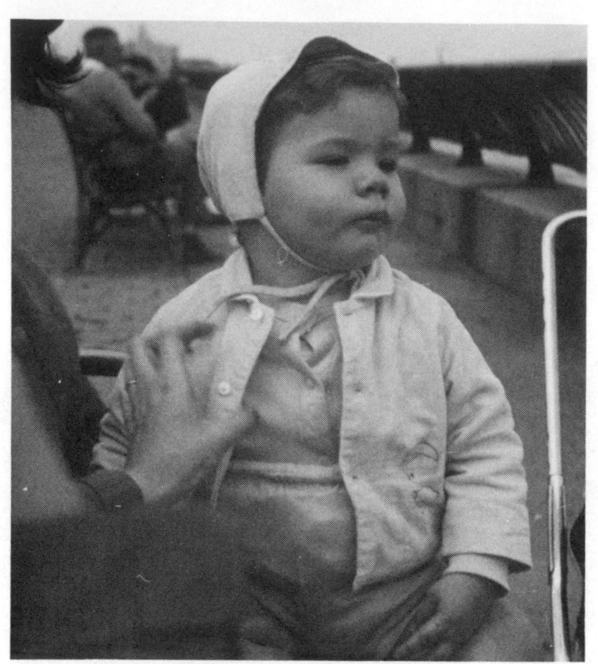

My second son, Arnim, in 1961.

Carlos in 1964.

A happy threesome in 1964.

In the Orient on a business trip with Peter.

known him to become violent in the presence of strangers, I was convinced he lacked the courage to force his way in. The baby-sitter was instructed to remain in the apartment with Arnim until further notice. I took Carlos to school every morning on my way to work, the school had instructions not to release him into the custody of Jan or anyone else, and I hired a special escort—in effect a bodyguard—to bring him home from school every afternoon. I had taken every precaution to insure our safety.

Two weeks after my brief confrontation with my husband I was awakened at 6:00 A.M. by the ringing of the telephone. Jan was calling to tell me he was leaving the United States permanently because the children and I wanted nothing more to do with him. I thought he was making another play for my sympathy and ended the conversation abruptly.

The next day the police called to tell me Jan had been killed in an automobile accident.

I was frozen.

The police called again, asking me to come to the hospital to identify the body. Jan had no other living relatives, so the task fell to me.

As I rode to the hospital in a taxi I suddenly remembered a passage from the Old Testament Book of Ezekiel that I had learned as a child, and, as far as I knew, had totally forgotten: *When a righteous man doth turn from his righteousness and commit iniquity and I lay a stumbling block before him, he shall die: because thou hast not given him warning, he shall die in his sin and his righteousness which he hath done shall not be remembered.*

I repeated the passage endlessly, hoping in vain that the words would endow me with a courage that was conspicuously lacking, but I was still in such a state of shock that I scarcely knew what they meant.

When we reached the hospital I threw some bills to the driver, blindly ran up the steps, then hesitated before I gathered the strength to ask for the morgue.

My feet felt like lead weights as I walked down a long, silent corridor.

An indifferent attendant barely glanced up from his desk when I timidly told him my mission. "Follow me," he said, and led me down another corridor to a door with a dirty glass window, which he pushed open.

I leaned against the door, began to weep and could not halt the flood of tears. I do not pretend now, any more than I did at the time, that I wept because of my loss. I had never loved Jan. He had made my life a torture for years, and I had hated him as I had never despised another human being.

I wept because I had been unable to help him. I wept for Arnim, who had lost his father. More than all else, I believe, I wept because a sudden sense of guilt overwhelmed me.

The impersonal voice of the attendant brought me back to reality. "Are you coming inside, lady?"

I wiped away my tears with the backs of my gloves and entered the morgue.

The attendant moved from slab to slab, checking name cards, and finally pulled back a sheet.

Jan's battered, lifeless face and body lay before me. Only his fine hands were intact, and I remember he was still wearing the wedding ring I had given him.

"Was this your husband, lady?"

I could only nod. Then I raced out of the room and down the corridor as though demons were pursuing me. Perhaps they were.

No sooner did I arrive home, exhausted after my ordeal, when the police telephoned again. In my panic I had neglected to sign the necessary identification papers and had to return to the morgue.

I was too tired to protest, and like a robot I went back to the morgue, where I endured the nightmare a second time.

Once at home again, I barely had the sense and energy to call a funeral parlor, which made all of the necessary arrangements.

Twelve people were present at the simple funeral. Arnim was still a baby, so I left him at home, but I took Carlos with me and tried to explain death to him. I did not weep again.

I thought my hell on earth was ended, but after I returned home I was besieged by an anxiety I had never before experienced. Suddenly I realized my own life was precious. I had to stay alive and keep healthy for the sake of my children. If anything happened to me, my sons would be given into the custody of foster parents—people who might not love them or appreciate them, people who might even abuse them.

My fear was morbid, I know, but it was very real to me and it haunted me for years, until I married Peter, my present husband.

I was afraid of being killed in a freak accident. I was afraid of contracting an incurable illness. How I struggled against those fears! When I became exhausted, the terror sometimes threatened to overcome me.

On such occasions I developed a special technique to

rid myself of them. I'd make an appointment with a doctor for a physical checkup, and after he assured me I was in the best of health I managed to relax again. For a time.

Those fears were Jan's legacy to me.

In the main, however, I felt relieved as the shock passed and I began to recover my equilibrium. Slowly the realization dawned that I was truly free at last. I had my sons. I had financial security. I was moving down the road toward American citizenship. I could make of my life what I pleased.

I made a vow never to marry again. I had had it with marriage.

Eight

My children were safe and happy. I no longer lived in fear for them or myself, and I celebrated by devoting new energies to my business future. I had already opened an extensive correspondence with some of my old contacts in South America, and now I began to write to others with whom I was dealing through the advertising agency. What I was seeking was the establishment of some new business venture.

Eventually I received an interesting letter from someone looking for a business partner in New York. Together we would finance and operate an export-import company, and I thought the basic concept was sound. I would be required to put up the sum of one hundred thousand dollars as my share of the original capital investment.

I had about twenty-five thousand in cash. I had bought another house in New York, and didn't want to add to the burdens of my real estate properties. I also owned some stocks, and believed I could obtain about forty thousand dollars as a loan from my bank by putting up those shares as collateral.

That left me short by thirty-five thousand, and after thinking about the problem at length I finally came up with the notion of trying to get it from my father.

My relations with my family were still poor. I wrote regularly to my parents, but neither of them ever replied, so I corresponded with my sister. I should say that I tried to correspond with her, and in my letters I asked if my father ever showed any interest in me, spoke of me or inquired about me.

Unfortunately, my sister was influenced by the attitudes of our parents, and her infrequent replies to my letters were cold, remote and uninformative. I found it hard to believe, however, that my father and mother were as indifferent toward me as they appeared.

What I didn't yet know was that my late husband had bombarded my father with letters. Following the same approach he had taken in his telephone calls to various people with whom I had been doing business, he fabricated wild stories about me, claiming I was dissolute, depraved and totally untrustworthy.

These lies were so farfetched that even my father was unable to believe them. He was infuriated, however, by the fact that I had married for a second time, as this was completely contrary to Spanish custom. In his eyes I had become a pariah.

Summoning my courage, I placed a telephone call to my father in Madrid. Our conversation was very brief. He told me I could blame no one but myself for marrying the wrong man, and he declared I had to take the consequences. He didn't stay on the line long enough to learn I was now a widow, and I had no opportunity to mention the reason for my call. He told me what he thought of me, then slammed down his telephone.

I was so startled I continued to hold my own telephone in my hand until I heard the international operator asking if I wanted to place another call. Then I dropped the instrument into its cradle and just stared into space, too numb to think or feel. I have no idea how long I sat there.

Carlos snapped me out of it. He came into the room, wanted to know what I was doing and why I was staring at the desk. When I made no reply he reminded me it was time for lunch, and that he and Arnim were hungry.

Of course. My children came first, and for their sake I couldn't wallow in self-pity. Whatever success I had achieved had been won on my own. Nothing in our situation was really changed, and I could not admit defeat simply because my father had rejected me again. It didn't take long to overcome my paralysis.

I had acquired two paintings which I was able to sell for six thousand dollars. I sold the diamond ring Jan had given me when we had been married, but I was still twenty thousand dollars shy of my goal. That left me no choice, so I took a big gamble and obtained a second mortgage on one of my real estate properties. I had to repay the principal in two years, and in the meantime I was also saddled with whopping interest payments. I was taking a tremendous risk for the sake of my new venture.

Armed with the capital, I went into business with my new partner, and began shipping British motorcars, whiskey and soap to South America.

I knew the returns would be slow, and I realized it would not be possible to earn large sums quickly in real estate, my other business. My job at the advertising agency gave me a security base, but perhaps that would have to be sacrificed too. The only way I could succeed would be through a rapid, large-scale expansion of the South American venture.

My assets were personal. I had confidence in my abilities. I had acquired some measure of standing in the financial community. I was free to lead my own life as I thought best. Above all, I believed that a woman, if she worked hard enough, could earn as much as any man.

I went to one of the leading Wall Street banks and had a long talk with the manager of the foreign department. He took my proposal seriously, which was refreshing, and he studied all of the facts I presented to him. Then he turned me down, saying that the South American countries with which I was dealing were politically unstable and I'd be wise to avoid that market.

I carried my plan to a second bank, and the same thing happened there. It dawned on me that banks were leery of overseas business in general and of South America in particular. So I was taking the wrong approach, and should sell my expansion idea to individuals rather than banks.

I wrote a thorough study of my present South American operation, plus a detailed breakdown of my expansion plans, including projected sales and earnings. I included biographical sketches of the people involved, both in New York and in Latin America. I was in no position to offer collateral, so I had to stress anticipated performance.

I sent the study to my first American business associate, the California shipbuilder. He was interested, and we discussed the deal in a series of long-distance telephone calls. The keys to my plan were my fresh ideas and the originality of the methods I was proposing. Eventually we reached an agreement, and he signed a two-year contract, opening a line of credit for me for a percentage of the profits. Now I was really in business on a comparatively large scale.

Three months later I had a call from my own bank. The official in charge of my account was so impressed by the results I was already achieving that he offered me additional credit!

I didn't need the money, but I nevertheless accepted. I reasoned that by using their credit I would establish closer relations with them. In the future it would be far easier for me to deal with them. As soon as I began taking money from them I voluntarily made periodic studies for them of programs already in effect. I was operating a small business, by bank standards, but I was able to give them the impression that I was efficient and knew what I was doing.

In the months that followed I led such a hectic life that my greatest problem was a lack of sleep. I thought myself lucky on a night when I could fall into bed for four hours. Organizing the South American business took up every moment I could devote to it, and I sent out reams of correspondence, doing my own typing because the letters had to be written in Spanish.

I had no personal life, and certainly no social life. There was no time to visit a beauty parlor, and my hair was a mess. I painted my nails in taxis or at bus stops, and even this was frivolous because I should have been using the time to make notes to myself or read correspondence. My few free hours on Sundays were spent in Central Park, where I played baseball with my sons. Needless to say, the sport was alien to me. Occasionally I managed to go bicycling, and in the spring I got up an hour early on Sundays to play tennis with a pro. My life was so sedentary I wanted to scream.

I had no opportunity to make long-range plans, and my lack of a social life was equally serious. I had gained an understanding of the American way of doing business, and knew that dinner parties were essential to the establishment of solid business contacts. If I truly wanted to expand, and my ambitions were limitless, I badly needed a larger circle of friends and acquaintances.

It was apparent to me that my job at the advertising agency was taking up too much of my time. I had to bring work home with me many nights, the pressures were relentless and I sometimes had to devote precious weekend time to agency problems. I should have quit much sooner than I did, but I wasn't actually as self-assured as I liked to believe.

I believed it vitally important, no matter what my own business enterprises, that I also hold a salaried position assuring me of a basic income. I was working for the purpose of earning a profit from my ventures, but I still had two small children to support in the event that I failed. Therefore I needed the feeling of security that a salary gave me. Without it I had no peace of mind; I fussed and fretted and worried, and couldn't give my full attention to the efforts that, if they succeeded, would bring in substantial sums.

I began to search for a part-time job that, if everything else failed, would still feed my sons and put a roof over their heads. After eight weeks I found it, and was hired by the College of Columbia University as an instructor in Spanish and Spanish literature. I had to be at work at 8:00 A.M. and stay until 12:00 noon, but this was a vast improvement over the hours my work at the advertising agency required.

I resigned from the agency and accepted the teaching post. My afternoons, evenings and weekends were my own, and almost overnight I had time to devote to my South American project without unduly straining myself. My schedule eased so dramatically that before long I was going to school early every morning so I could swim in the huge pool there. This took care of my craving for physical exercise.

Soon I also found fulfillment for my need for male companionship. I met a young diplomat in his early thirties and was attracted by his lively features and deep blue eyes. We attended a number of parties together, flirted mildly and had a very pleasant semi-romance. I wasn't ready for an affair; he had no desire for a lasting relationship either, and we simply enjoyed each other's company. Our friendship ended suddenly when he received an overnight transfer to a post in Europe.

Next came a banker, also in his thirties. He was a handsome bachelor. Personable. We dated frequently, but he had a major flaw. He had developed an insistent interest in marriage, which was the last thing on earth I wanted.

As I became increasingly restless I realized I wanted and needed sex, but I had no intention of giving myself to any man who might come along. I needn't be in love, but I refused to go to bed with a man I was dating casually. Several casuals appeared, one after the other, filling the void in my life, but I soon discovered that each of them was not for me. Some women instinctively recognize a man who is right for them, but as my record indicates, I was never a member of that intuitive breed. Most of the men I dated would have been dreadfully wrong.

I was searching for a man who was wise, personable, strong and gentle, a man who would love me but one who would understand why I shrank from marriage. He never showed up. I taught my college classes, I worked on my own projects, I took care of my children. I was so hungry for the right man in my life that I wanted to cry, but I couldn't shed a tear.

I tried in vain to analyze myself. Why couldn't I find someone who suited me? Well, men of my own age were fun but superficial. They hadn't yet learned how to treat a woman who had become an adult, and soon each of them bored me. Oh well, better luck next time.

I am sparked sexually only by men who are intelligent and who also have the other good qualities I wanted, and they also must have worldly experience and savoir faire. In other words, I realized I wanted an older man, and that I was still hunting for a father substitute. Not a healthy attitude.

My dates seemed to fall into a pattern. After the get-acquainted period, we'd go to dinner, then to the theater or dancing. Kisses and more kisses. Back to his apartment, with still more kisses in the elevator. Most of these men lived in buildings with elevator operators, and I was always embarrassed by these public demonstrations of affection. No matter; kisses in elevators were *de rigeur*.

When we reached his apartment I anticipated love-making that would sweep my protests under his rug. Instead there were bone-chilling preliminaries.

The most common was the neatness excuse. "I don't know how this place got into such a mess. She just moved out last week."

I didn't give a damn when she had moved out.

Sometimes there was the oblique reference approach. "My ex-wife, Mrs. Parkings . . ."

An ex-wife was always called Mrs.—never Mary or Helen or Jean. Apparently these ladies never had first names.

Then there was the play for sympathy. "I thought I married a girl of compassion and understanding, but I was wrong."

By this point in the conversation I became irritated. "In other words," I said, "you married a fraud."

What violent protests! Invariably the former wife had been a paragon who had then changed—for inexplicable reasons.

Of course she had been perfect. If she had been flawed, the husband's failure to recognize it would have been a negative reflection of his judgment, and the male ego never permits admission of an error. By this time I was beginning to yawn and glance surreptitiously at my watch.

Next came the gratuitous pitch. "Now, thanks to you, I can be myself."

I nodded my thanks, and waited for the line I knew was coming: The Test of a Woman's Intentions.

"You wouldn't believe it, but this place has looked like a supermarket. Canned goods piled up all over the kitchen and the freezer overflowing with frozen foods."

Just before reaching for my coat and shoulderbag I delivered the coup de grace. "Well, you needn't worry that I'd ever cook for you, because I don't know how. I've always refused to be buried under a pile of domestic debris."

So much for that pseudo-romance, and on to the next. I was expected to supply peace and harmony, exciting sex and fresh foods cooking. Instead I said nasty, cruel things that reminded the poor man of his former wife. On the infrequent occasions that we progressed far enough for it, sex was mutually unsatisfactory. It could not have been otherwise, given the lack of compatibility.

I told myself I was demanding a degree of perfection that didn't exist in men. I was being too critical, too demanding. So I'd try again.

Soon I became aware of a basic law in American society: A widow with two small children was incapable of attracting bachelors. All of the men who came into my life were divorced, separated or still married; in which case they didn't see me again. Some were widowers with children of their own. Some, who were divorced, had custody of their children.

I had no intention of submitting my own children to the vagaries of my dating, which meant I rarely brought a man home with me. Besides, I lost my mobility if *he* came to *my* place.

I remember some of my beaux with affection tinged with amusement. One was Julius, a widower with two sons, aged thirteen and ten. "My life is disorganized," Julius often said, and had no idea how accurate was his description.

After a pleasant dinner somewhere we'd return to Julius' apartment, and find the living room cluttered with guitars, records, toy soldiers and four or five preteens. Instead of sending his sons off to bed at night, Julius and I would sit making conversation with the youngsters until they became sleepy. To this day I'm convinced those children rarely slept.

Ultimately I'd be obliged to use the bathroom, and that was when my stomach turned. Julius and his sons had no understanding of even the rudiments of cleanliness, and it was obvious that the cleaning woman who came in daily was forbidden to go near the bathroom. A filthy wash basin; towels and underwear and rubbish thrown everywhere!

Invariably I felt compelled to scrub the sink and put the place in order. By that time the aftereffects of a pleasant dinner had worn off, and I was ready to go home by the fastest taxi available. Good-bye, Julius.

Next, was a character who really had me puzzled. I still don't know what I found attractive in him. He was a collector of stamps and of beer mugs bearing such inspiring labels as "Disneyland" and "Yosemite National Park." On one special occasion he actually allowed me to hold some seashells he had picked up on Cape Cod.

He relished telling me in infinite detail about his fishing trips, and couldn't grasp the fact, which I tried to drop subtly, that fishing bores me. I am not turned on by camping out and cooking clams by moonlight. Never mind, he and I would go off together for a glorious honeymoon without marriage.

Where did he suggest?

"A fishing camp I know in the Catskills."

My lack of enthusiasm must have communicated itself to him.

So he tried again. "We could go for a weekend in a foreign country."

What country did he have in mind?

"Puerto Rico."

Good-bye, collector of stamps and beer mugs.

Next came a man I'll call Tony, with whom I had a real affair. Only in retrospect do I realize that our relationship was based on my imagination rather than his real qualities, and that I was repeating old patterns, old mistakes.

Tony was tall, slender and silent. He rarely made small talk, which made him unlike other American men I had known, and I'm certain that was the quality that drew me to him. Most men jabbered, but Tony listened. He was wealthy, a member of a prominent family. However, he had no pretensions. Even in those pre-jeans days he liked to wear jeans and old sweaters with holes in them.

He was a marvelous listener who almost never said anything inconsequential and hardly ever smiled. "Mr. Stern" is what I called him, and my efforts to persuade or cajole him to relax usually failed. Tony had reduced his entire life to a schedule, and even made love only at predetermined times—on Thursday nights and Saturday afternoons.

Once, after telling my children I had to go out of town on a business trip, I spent an entire night with Tony. New York was hit with a snowstorm, and it was still snowing the next morning as we ate breakfast.

Tony became positively loquacious. "Stay pretty forever," he said. "Always be young. Keep that perfect grooming."

I stared at him, my stomach churning. "The way I am right this minute?" I asked, trying to sound calm.

"Well, no. You aren't wearing makeup, and your hair is rather messy."

I almost choked on my coffee. Tony was the voice of my family, and of my first husband. Only a facade was important. My mind and personality, my ideals, goals and ambitions were inconsequential. Shades of the nineteenth century! I was a toy—a doll whose sole purpose in life was to provide entertainment for a male.

Good-bye, Tony.

Other aspects of life came first.

For me, romance would have to wait. I rationalized that this penchant I had for choosing the wrong types was my way of avoiding the issue altogether. It was more than likely that, as much as I wanted romance, I was afraid to accept it. Other aspects of my life had to come first.

Nine

During Columbia's summer recess and Christmas and Easter holidays I would make trips to South America to supervise that end of the export-import business. I had my work cut out for me. My partner was an amiable, honest and hard-working man, but he reminded me of the major cities of South America, which grew without planning and sprawled all over the place. That's how our business grew. My partner was unable to plan.

Too often he gave in to enthusiasms of the moment, which meant our warehouses were filled to overflowing with unsold merchandise. Too often he ordered merchandise that was difficult to sell, and then we carried a heavy inventory instead of making a quick profit. I tried to curb his buying, both in person and on the telephone, but I had my hands full. Our arguments were friendly because we were showing a handsome profit.

My real estate ventures were prospering too, and I was making money on my stocks. I paid my debts without strain, and perhaps I should have been satisfied with my life. Instead, I was restless, afraid of being frozen into a corner and still wanting to accomplish much more. The curse of ambition may be less deadly than that of inertia, but it doesn't make a happy life.

On my trips to South America I kept my eyes and ears open, and repeatedly investigated possible outlets for expansion. I found companies that I believed would succeed if new capital was infused into them, and I came across others that needed reorganization. None appealed to me. I bided my time, and I wish I could say I exercised patience, but I didn't. Instead, I fumed, cursed myself for "wasting" time and was miserable. I'm not the first to discover that we make our own hell in the world.

During this period I made a major domestic step. I purchased a small co-op apartment in New York and moved into it with my children. The co-op was a symbol of my success, and even more important, offered my children and me greater security. I should have been very pleased and proud. I'm slightly ashamed to admit that I took the place for granted. My horizons had expanded, and I'm sorry to say that not until much later did I finally recognize its significance.

Making money had become my obsession, and I was frantically busy. Even though the various business opportunities I unearthed in South America were of no direct interest to me, I refussd to let them be wasted. Sometimes I arranged loans and was given a commission in cash or in stock. I persuaded American friends and acquaintances to invest in various South American projects. This wasn't easy. Most people I knew were afraid to put money into South America, where many businessmen didn't know the meaning of ethics. I was fortunate, however, and no bank, no individual ever lost a penny in Latin America as a result of taking my advice.

One venture in particular worked out well. A company in which friends invested became profitable very quickly, and I earned a substantial commission. Then I interested a group of Japanese businessmen in the corporation, and when they purchased it the investors made still more, while I earned a second, larger commission.

Everything I did was business-oriented. Other women might read popular books and magazines for pleasure or relaxation; I read the *Wall Street Journal, Fortune* and *Business Week*. I had always appreciated the value of grooming, and I began to buy expensive clothes and accessories, not out of vanity, but because I wanted my business colleagues to see at a glance that I was successful. In business the facade of success means everything.

Without consciously realizing it I was becoming an expert on South American business, and even my acquaintances in banking began coming to me for advice and information. I knew I had arrived when an official of a major bank asked my help in organizing a new corporation based on the commercial and industrial potentials of various South American countries.

On December 21, 1963, the children and I moved into our new home. I had been so busy that not until I actually took possession did I realize it was shabby and neglected. The bathroom fixtures were old, layer upon layer of wallpaper decorated the walls, and dirt was everywhere.

Only the beds were moved in that day, and I sat down on a trunk to figure out what had to be done first. Carlos drove me to distraction by standing beside me, saying, "Mummy, where's the Christmas tree? Where is it?"

First I bought the tree, then I got to work. At first I thought I'd do my own decorating, but after figuring what my time was worth by the hour I realized I was being foolish and hired a decorator to supervise everything, including the work of the plumbers, carpenters and painters. I gave her a budget and the freedom to do as she pleased, provided she kept a love of antiques in mind and used those I already owned.

Day by day the significance of owning that apartment increased. It dawned on me that I wanted to sink deep roots there, to create a beautiful, gracious home for my children and me, and a place where I could entertain to my business advantage.

When my home was ready it was lovely, and I appreciated it, but I took no time off to relax in it. Instead I began to use it for small business dinners, meetings and cocktail parties. I was too compulsive to think in any other terms.

The increasing volume of my South American work took up more and more of my time, sometimes making it necessary for me to leave Columbia when school was in session. By this time I didn't actually need the lifeline of my job there, but I couldn't admit that to myself, so I sometimes hired a fill-in instructor to take my place at my lectures.

It was easy for me to see faults in other women. I had known a number of females in advertising and in teaching who held the same jobs for year after year, never advancing and seemingly content in the same rut. I crit icized them privately, telling myself their lack of incentive was responsible for their lack of mobility.

Yet I was unable to cut my own ties with the university!

In the 1950s and 1960s, before the achievements of the women's liberation movement, it was very difficult for a woman to move ahead in a man's world. Hard work is a primary ingredient, but long-range planning is another. I planned with care and urged my friends in teaching and advertising to do the same.

"List your assets," I told them. "Ask yourself where you'll be in a year, and in five years. Will this satisfy you? If not, how can you improve your position? If your job doesn't fulfill your inner needs, start thinking about another—and how to get it."

Again and again I told them, "You're smarter than you think!"

Women who try to make their way in a world of men are inclined to be too modest and diffident, and more often than not place too low a value on their abilities. I frequently experimented in my classes at Columbia to prove my point. First I'd ask the girls to rate their intelligence, and was not surprised when those who were above average called themselves average. Then I asked the same question of young men who were less intelligent than the girls, and with the supreme confidence of their sex they almost always replied, "Above average."

Certainly it does no harm and may be helpful for a woman to use her femininity in business. I did, without regrets.

In the 1960s I found myself having almost daily business lunches with men. I must admit it was sometimes difficult for me to determine whether a man was interested in me as a business associate or as a woman. All things being equal, it was easier for me to set up a lunch date with a man I wanted to see than it would have been had I been a male instead of a female.

So many of these men made verbal passes at me during the first fifteen minutes of a business lunch that I became expert at turning them down. However, I was infuriated when one of them came back by calling me frigid. It is astonishing how many of them made that accusation. I was forced to conclude that they never looked at themselves in the mirror. Apparently every man fancies himself a Clark Gable or Robert Redford, and assumes something must be wrong with a woman when he can't make it with her.

All I can say is that I was proud and inaccessible when I had been a penniless immigrant, uncertain where I'd find the money to pay for my baby's next meal. I was equally proud and inaccessible when I had proven myself in the world. The men I met for lunch knew my earnings were large, and my clothes as well as my reputation told them I was no poor working girl, dependent on the crumbs they might deign to throw me. But still they tried. It must be the nature of the beast.

Most of them, however, subsided when I turned them off. Then it was strictly up to me to interest them in the business venture that we had come together to discuss. Many of them quickly developed respect for my determination and whatever skill I possessed, and were intrigued both by what I said and my reasons for saying it.

Occasionally it became plain to me that the man I was

meeting hadn't been interested in business from the outset and still had other things on his mind. On these occasions I reverted to my profession as a teacher and taught them lessons. Sometimes I delivered a general lecture on the importance of business in our society. Or, if I was in the mood, I made an address on tax structures, always stressing the importance to the consumer of tax reductions. I was sincere in what I said, and sometimes a man who had met me with only sex in mind came back to me later and invited me to participate in some business enterprise with him. Every woman must earn respect in her own way.

In the early 1960s I began to develop an interest in commodities, particularly when I realized there was a growing shortage of many raw materials. I began to keep extensive files on people who dealt in sugar, copra, tobacco, oil, cotton and other raw materials. Commodities are speculative investments, but I thought I should have a sprinkling in my portfolio. After thorough scrutiny, I made a few purchases of commodities directly in their home countries. I made sure that none were under the direct control of those governments. What I was doing was educating myself, taking a course in commodities so I would understand them when shortages became more acute.

Not all of my investments were successful, and sometimes I took a beating, but I was learning. One unsuccessful venture distressed me more than others because it was a joint venture in which a woman who was a good friend lost a sum of money that was important to her. I was better able to absorb my loss.

At the 1964 New York World's Fair, I saw some Spanish art objects made of inlaid wood that fascinated me, and I learned the exquisite work was being done by two men who were going blind because such meticulous craftsmanship was required. I decided to buy these objects and start a new export-import company.

My friend, who is a painter, shared my enthusiasm and joined me as my partner. In our eagerness we neglected to do basic market research, and this neglect proved fatal. First we took the objects to art galleries, but the owners told us they couldn't sell them, and suggested we try the furniture marts. The furniture people turned us down and said we should go to art galleries.

I didn't want to let my friend down, so I arranged a joint exhibit for her paintings and the inlaid wood. Still they didn't sell, principally because they were too expensive, and between us we still own a number to the present day. Worst of all, both of us were career women, and we could ill afford the time we spent trying to dispose of the stock.

The venture taught me a crucial lesson. I would never do business with friends. If a deal fails, one can lose a friend. Even if it succeeds, the friend, if inexperienced, often expects to earn larger profits. Business and personal relations simply don't mix.

By 1965, life had become very pleasant. I was solvent, earning a very comfortable living, and satisfied with my vocational progress. My sons were healthy, active boys endowed with so much energy they exhausted me. I tried to be a father as well as a mother to them, and on weekends I played ball, ran races and generally succeeded in knocking myself out.

My love life was nonexistent. I still think of 1965 as

the Year of the Drunkards. I never touch alcohol, not even wine, and never have, because I don't care for either the taste or the effects. That year, it seems, every man I met was a heavy drinker. I didn't get along with any of them.

By this time I was seeing a number of married couples who invited me to dinner parties. One of these women became a good friend and decided to take the responsibility for finding an interesting man with whom I would be compatible. I was amused by her efforts and didn't take them seriously.

One night at about ten o'clock, when I was reading in bed, I received an emergency telephone call from her. An after-theater party was developing at her house, and as too many men were gathering there, she desperately needed extra women. Would I be a dear and hurry over?

She was a close friend, and it did sound like fun. So I dressed and made up hurriedly and took a taxi to her house. I was doing her a favor, and the next morning I would regret the lack of sleep—or so I thought. It didn't cross my mind that I might meet a man who would interest me.

Paul and I took to each other at first sight. He was charming, attractive and intelligent. He was also twenty years my senior. It was the older-man syndrome again. We talked for hours, and I eagerly accepted his dinner invitation for the next night.

The relationship that developed seemed almost too good to be true. Paul was genuinely interested in me. What I thought and felt and did were important to him. Sex had its place, and we enjoyed it thoroughly, but it didn't outweigh the other aspects of our friendship. Best of all—and I regarded this as almost miraculous—Paul accepted without question or argument my insistence that I had no intention of marrying him.

He and my children developed strong, mutual affections, and often he visited them or took them on outings when I was working. He wasn't trying to impress me, but saw them because he and they had fun together. At last there was a father substitute in my sons' lives—as well as in mine.

I was more contented than I had ever been in my life, and my happiness was doubled when I became an American citizen. Only one aspect of my life was incomplete: I wanted to mend relations with my parents.

By this time my father had become my reluctant partner in several business deals, having found it impossible to resist the urge to engage in ventures he knew would be profitable. But his correspondence with me was totally impersonal, and I knew I had not been forgiven for my independence. He had been responsible for instilling that spirit in me, and I was ever-conscious of the irony.

Late in the summer of 1965 I went to Spain, armed with my new, green passport and hoping against hope that a separation of eleven years had wrought a change in my parents' attitude toward me. For symbolic reasons I flew to Madrid on an American airline.

My father had so many connections that, had he cared to exert himself slightly, he and my mother could have been waiting for me at the foot of the ramp when I disembarked from the airplane. When I didn't see them standing there I knew I was in for a rough time.

I found them awaiting me in the back seat of their chauffeur-driven car. My mother gave me a cool cheek to kiss, and my father completed the ritual by placing a cold kiss on my cheek. No sooner was I settled in the back seat between them than he launched into a discussion of business. I might have been a stranger.

My mother inspected me curiously and with great care, searching my face and weighing the price of my clothes and accessories. Finally she passed judgment. "I don't like your false eyelashes," she said.

When we reached the house I walked through the door and regressed ten years into the past. The dark, heavy furniture was unchanged, and immediately depressed me. The same servants were on their staff, still endowed with the same formal, old-fashioned attitudes. Accustomed to the breeziness of American living, I felt stifled.

I wanted to call New York to let the children know I had arrived safely, and one of the servants was shocked when I dialed the operator myself. I might break a fingernail.

I wanted a glass of orange juice, and my mother was mildly astonished when I started to go to the kitchen for it. "Why have servants if you must do such things for yourself?" she asked.

At our first dinner together they agreed I looked well but made no inquiries about my way of life, my home or my work. They asked politely after Carlos, but made no mention of Arnim, and it dawned on me that in this house the child of my second marriage was taboo. To them he didn't exist. Obviously I had to be careful of what I said under their roof.

I brought them a suitcase filled with presents—that

thawed the ice. Or, I should say, the presents opened the floodgates. My mother, still a hypochondriac, told me in excruciating detail about her many ailments. My father, still a worrier, explained at length why his world might collapse at any moment.

My sister was married, and the barrier she had erected between us did not come down. I found her husband pleasant but remote.

I tried to escape into the company of old friends, and discovered a strange phenomenon. The girls who had been pretty had married sad nonentities. Those who had been ugly had married virile, personable and ambitious men who were making something of their lives. A number of my old friends snubbed me because, as I quickly learned, my first husband had convinced them that I had been guilty of infidelity, and that this had been the cause of our break.

Although no one said it in so many words, relatives as well as friends believed Carlos was not my husband's son, and the cause of my abrupt departure from Spain. The following year, when I brought him to Spain with me, my aunts, uncles and cousins were astonished by his resemblance to his father. I couldn't resist commenting that I felt sure they were disappointed.

I had planned to spend three weeks in Madrid, the longest vacation I had taken in ten years, but after the first week I found time hanging heavily on my hands. I spent the next two weeks learning as much as I could about my father's various businesses. He was surprised by my ability to grasp essentials quickly, and this amused me as he appeared to have forgotten he had been my teacher.

I felt no pain when I left Madrid at the end of my

three-week stay. The country had progressed economically, but in other respects, particularly in her customs and attitudes toward religion, she was still the Spain of the Middle Ages. Unlike so many immigrants to the United States, I found it easy to cut the umbilical cord that tied me to my native country. Spain had given me my pride and my love of art. In all other respects I had become an American.

My trip to Spain did produce one positive result. I had reestablished relations with my family. Granted that I hadn't been received into the fold as a daughter, but I told myself that I would be dealing with my father in various business matters in the future, and something was better than nothing. My parents were growing old, which saddened me, but I now knew they were incapable of loving me, and I faced reality.

My future was in America.

Ten

Soon after I returned to the United States I resumed my travels, this time going to South America to look after my business interests. Our expansion in several countries had been so rapid that it had been difficult for us to make thorough credit investigations of the people with whom we were dealing, and sometimes they proved to be poor risks. Until now the drain on our income had been minor, but I didn't want to suffer a major loss before taking steps to lock the barn door. I bought a finance company that would provide service for our clients, and in this way made certain we wouldn't suffer.

After I went back to New York I continued to expand my Latin American operations. By now I could afford to move at a cautious pace because I no longer had to earn large sums of money quickly. Eventually I became associated with a company in Brazil and began shipping merchandise there. Brazil had been growing more rapidly than any other developing country, with the result that manufactured goods of all kinds were in great demand there. This venture prospered from the start.

I hadn't yet achieved a complete sense of inner security, even though my business affairs were in good shape, so I continued to teach at Columbia. Sometimes I told myself I was wasting valuable time, but I couldn't and wouldn't allow myself to resign. Not until later did I finally realize I didn't want to quit. I was enjoying my relations with undergraduates, and their outlook on life kept me young. What's more, they were the consumers of tomorrow, and it was important to know what they thought and what they wanted in life. The insights I gained were well worth the twenty hours per week that I spent at the school.

I continued to enjoy a very pleasant personal relationship with Paul. Sometimes I thought I loved him, while at other times I knew better, but at the very least I felt deep affection for him.

Troubles started to surface after we had gone together for about three years. He began to suffer from increasingly deep depression, and it hurt me to see him in such anguish. As I had known for a long time, he had been in psychotherapy for many years.

I can't begin to count the hours I spent, either in person or on the telephone, trying to improve his frame of mind. I realized my efforts were a failure; if a professional psychiatrist couldn't help him, there was little or nothing I could do for him, but still I had to try. It was impossible for me to stand aside and do nothing while he slid down a mental manhole.

For the third time in my life, I found myself associated with someone who was emotionally ill. Once again I had demonstrated my genius for becoming involved with a man who would cause trouble for me. The fault was my own, and I should have known better. Let me go back to the beginning of my relationship with Paul.

We went together for a week before he held my hand. Not until the end of the second week did he kiss me. Then, with this barrier down, he began to caress me, sometimes by the hour, but never went any further. Night after night I became aroused and was left dangling. He invariably stopped short of the sexual act, even when I became so desperate that I demanded it.

At first he presented excuses. He had worked hard and was tired. There were serious problems on his mind that made it impossible for him to function physically. Then the excuses stopped, but the pattern remained unchanged.

Some nights I was so worked up that I would have gone to bed with almost any man who had come along. On a number of occasions, after I returned home from a petting session, I was so aroused I was tempted to telephone some other man and urge him to join me without delay. Fortunately I was able to restrain myself.

Sex with other men was too easy to attain. I thrived on challenges, and Paul represented a challenge.

After several months, when I told him flatly that something had to be done, he confessed to me that he believed himself to be impotent. This was difficult for me to accept, but he gave me no real choice.

One morning I could tolerate no more. It was a hot day, with the dusty smell of summer coming in through the open door of the lobby, where I was sitting while the building doorman summoned a taxi for me. I jumped to my feet, glanced at the beady-eyed pigeons on the sidewalk and caught a glimpse of the cloudless blue sky. It occurred to me that I wanted Paul so badly I was going out of my mind. Not just any man, but Paul.

I understood him, or thought I did. He was frightened of sex, perhaps with any woman and certainly with me. I had reached a stage that caused me to wonder whether I was losing my attractiveness—and I had to prove that I was still desirable.

My craving for Paul was too acute, too overwhelming to be denied. I had to have him without delay, that very morning. I yearned for him so intensely that I knew I would have no peace of mind until we went to bed together.

I made no attempt to rid myself of this mood, and dismissing an appointment at Columbia from my agenda, I gave the taxi driver the address of Paul's apartment. I knew I had succumbed to a temporary insanity and tried to ask myself whether Paul was worth my effort, but I couldn't even answer the question sensibly.

I was frightened and confused, never before had I been the aggressor in sex, but I was determined to become intimate with Paul if I had to attack him physically in order to achieve my goal. There was no other way to restore my equilibrium.

My ardor cooled a trifle when I stood in front of his apartment door and raised my hand to ring the bell. I would be crushed and humiliated if he rejected me. Perhaps I should leave well enough alone, enjoy his companionship and seek sex elsewhere. If I had any brains, any sensitivity, I would turn and run.

I paced up and down the narrow corridor outside his apartment, in my agitation, brushing against the wall the way an upset lioness rubs against the bars of her cage. In my ferment I literally couldn't make up my mind.

All at once I heard the voice of a woman behind the closed door.

Aha!

I had been here before. It was my first husband all over again. Like him, Paul was sleeping with someone else while pretending to love me.

At that point nothing would persuade me to run away. When I find a business deal has gone sour I make a clean break and write it off. I had to do the same with Paul. Only by confronting him, face to face, would I be able to overcome my desire for him. I needed the satisfaction of telling him off, letting him know in no uncertain terms that he wasn't worthy of my love.

I stopped abruptly in front of the door and rang the bell.

After a long wait Paul opened the door, and he was wearing only his pajamas. I saw red.

Then behind him in the living room, I caught a glimpse of a middle-aged cleaning woman vacuuming the rug.

In that instant my jealousy vanished. My desire for Paul returned with a rush, and with it I felt a sense of tenderness toward him that was unique.

Paul read my expression, and didn't need to ask why I had come to him. He handed the maid a twenty-dollar bill and asked her to return the following morning.

We didn't speak, and I don't think either of us moved while we waited for the woman to leave. The instant the door closed behind her we embraced, both of us laughing and trembling.

I wasted no time. Pushing him backward onto the sofa, I caressed him wildly as I tore off his pajamas, telling him repeatedly that I loved him and couldn't wait any longer for him.

If he had been impotent earlier in our relationship he enjoyed an instantaneous cure that morning.

Later, after we were satiated, we talked with a new frankness. Paul admitted he had been suffering anxieties because of the twenty-two-year difference in our ages.

I protested that I didn't care, but I wasn't telling the truth. If I had been as indifferent to that age gap as I indicated, I would have been willing to marry him.

Nevertheless I believed I loved him, and promised him it would be "forever."

Wiser and more cautious than I, Paul suggested we allow the long-range future to take care of itself. We had sex again before I finally went off to Columbia.

Thereafter I behaved like an adolescent in love. I daydreamed about Paul, thinking by the hour about the way he looked, the way he moved, the way he talked, the way he made love. I was miserable when I was separated from him. I telephoned him at odd hours. I even neglected my work for his sake, something I had never done.

Fortunately for both of us this phase didn't last long. However, I had a far deeper understanding of Paul. I realized he was an exceptionally complex man, and I began to know those complexes, quickly recognizing the symptoms when he fell prey to anxiety or depression.

I came to know his guilts, and I scolded him, trying to force him to overcome them. These efforts were doomed from the outset, although I refused to admit as much to myself.

My attachment to him became deeper. Our physical relations were perfect, and became one of the strongest ties that bound us together. I grew still closer to him emotionally, as well, so that—in a sense—his problems became mine.

I threw myself into our relationship with the zeal I had demonstrated only in business, and we became almost suffocatingly close. I was trying to will him into a new, permanent state of mind, refusing to recognize that I was seeking the impossible.

For a time Paul was vastly improved, and I convinced myself that I had made him well again. I would have married him, but he knew himself far better than I knew him, and he refused. Under no circumstances would he ever allow himself to become a burden on me. When I assured him he was no burden, he merely smiled.

Gradually, almost imperceptibly over the years, Paul's problems began to take hold of him again. For a long time our sex relations remained ideal, but in other ways he started to slip back into the well of depression.

I fought these tendencies in him, but this was one battle I couldn't win. Little by little Paul's charm vanished beneath a blanket of anxieties and despondency, and his gaity gave way to a permanent gloom.

I refused to admit defeat, and insisted I would cure him. I would do what no psychiatrist could. Even now, years later, I can't help wondering whether all of my concern was genuine. Perhaps I was acting, at least part of the time, because I enjoyed playing the role of a noble heroine. I don't like suffering, and it is inconceivable to me that I allowed myself to suffer so long and so hard for his sake.

I tried to prepare myself mentally for disaster that seemed inevitable. My thinking was complicated by periods of improvement: At times Paul thoroughly enjoyed himself, and I became at least temporarily convinced that he was on the mend.

One fact stood out above all others: As his illness progressed he clung to me more and more tenaciously, and as his need for me increased we drew still closer.

I was much more than his mistress. I became his caretaker, his nurse, even his doctor during periods when he capriciously refused to see his psychiatrist. I still loved him, or thought I did, so there was no escape for me. I was convinced that if I left him he would do away with himself.

My own life was becoming miserable, but there was nothing I could do to alleviate it. My pain was ever-present, and on the rare occasions when I wanted to rebel I knew I couldn't. Paul was incapable of survival without me.

By the latter part of 1967, when he had returned to his psychiatrist for treatment, the realization gradually dawned on me that I was doing Paul no good. In spite of my devotion to him he was still inching his way downhill.

I persuaded him to allow me to have a private talk with his psychiatrist, and at last he consented.

The doctor, who was a self-assured man, asked me to temper my demands on Paul so I wouldn't interfere with his delicately complex psychotherapeutic program.

If I understood the psychiatrist correctly, he was asking me to leave Paul so I wouldn't stand between him and the doctor's goals. When I asked if my interpretation was correct, the psychiatrist nodded.

I well knew that Paul had been going to him for treatment over a period of many years, and had shown no real improvement during that time. I held back nothing, and made my thinking clear.

The reply was predictable. Without psychiatric support, Paul would fall completely apart.

I asked if that same thing might happen if I left him, and whether Paul might commit suicide.

The psychiatrist waved aside my fears. He knew his patient and could control him.

That ended our meeting, and I was filled with doubts and fears as I walked out to the street.

Analyzing Paul's situation, I knew the psychiatrist had not helped him in ten long years of treatment. Perhaps my thinking was colored by my dislike of the man, but that night I suggested to Paul that he might fare better if he went to another psychiatrist.

He refused, his eyes filled with fear.

He was so close to complete panic that I refrained from making the same suggestion again.

But the time had come for me to reorganize my own life. Perhaps Paul was helpless, but I was not. Perhaps the psychiatrist was right, and I should leave him. Certainly that was the sensible thing for me to do for my own sake, if not for his.

Even now I cannot dwell on the tremendous effort I made or the toll it took. I struggled for many weeks, my torment worse than any I had ever known, and finally, in a burst of desperation, I told Paul I couldn't see him again.

He accepted the break, but continued to telephone me. This was no real termination of our relationship, as I well knew, but at least I was no longer seeing him. My children and I were relatively free again.

One night, during a long conversation, Paul revealed to me that he was seeing a second psychotherapist while still having his regular meetings with the first. His answer was evasive when I asked if the first doctor approved, and he rambled at length without making much sense when I asked what he hoped to accomplish.

Perhaps I was being harsh, but it seemed to me he didn't want to be cured, and actually enjoyed being the center of so much attention. I made up my mind to stop having these pointless telephone conversations with him. I was doing him no good and was tearing myself open again. I told him my decision, and again he agreed.

After a month of silence he called me abruptly one Sunday afternoon and asked me to marry him.

I refused, sympathetically and gently.

Then he began to ramble, calling me mysterious and Machiavellian, and saying I wanted to destroy any man who came into my life.

If I was that kind of a person, I said, I couldn't imagine why he wanted to marry me.

He didn't bother to listen, and instead told me I didn't know what I wanted. I demanded a father relationship with a man, he declared, but refused to be submissive to it.

Never during the three years of our relationship had he wanted me to be submissive to him. On the contrary, it was he who had clung to me, demanding that I provide the strength he lacked.

I realized he was trying to blame me for his problems, including his sexual tensions and unreliability. I refused to accept his nonsense, and asked him not to spoil the good we had known together by saying things that weren't true.

By refusing him, he said, I alone would be to blame for the future. Suddenly the line went dead.

It wasn't like Paul to be gruff, authoritarian and peevish, and his strange call made me uneasy. I tried to puzzle it out, and suddenly I realized he had been threatening to kill himself.

I called him back, but there was no answer.

Hurriedly I grabbed a coat and ran to his apartment. The doorman told me he had gone out.

I called Paul's sister, who said she hadn't heard from him. She shared my alarm. Between us, in the next few hours, we called everyone who had been associated with him for many years. He had called no one, seen no one. Every quarter of an hour I tried his apartment again, but the phone just rang.

By early evening I had to give up, not knowing where else to turn. I sat with my sons while they ate dinner, but had no appetite myself. My fears had increased, and my apprehensions became unbearable. I still cared for Paul, and I was so worried I felt physically ill. Ultimately I went to bed, refusing to give in to the urge to take a sleeping pill. Instinct told me I needed to be clearheaded.

One week later the tragic news hit me via the phone in the middle of the night. Carlos picked up the exten sion at the same time I answered the phone in my bedroom.

Then, hiding his own sorrow, this twelve-year-old boy who was so mature for his age came in to my bedroom to console me. He refused to leave my side for the rest of the long night, and only his presence made it possible for me to control the hysteria that welled up in me. Again, Carlos had been there when I needed him.

I suffered more that night and in the days that followed than ever before in my life. My grief over Paul was complicated by overwhelming guilts. For the second time a man who had loved me had been killed. Was I really a man-eating bitch who drove men to suicide? I didn't know, but I suspected the worst.

As my initial numbness passed I became introspective, and once again I analyzed my strengths and weaknesses, my attitudes and conduct. For three years I had given Paul my love and my emotional, intellectual and spiritual support, asking little in return.

Gradually I rid myself of my guilts, realizing it was wrong to blame myself for Paul's death.

My flaw was quite different. Twice I had been drawn to weak men who already had strong suicidal tendencies. Twice I had paid for my mistake, and I vowed never to repeat the error. Never again could I allow myself to become seriously involved with any man who lacked stability and strength of character.

I continued to grieve for poor, helpless Paul, but I put our three years together into the past. At no time had I neglected my children or my work, but now they demanded my undivided energy and attention.

Eleven

Early in 1968 I began to feel familiar pangs of conscience, with an inner voice telling me I was stagnating and wasting my time. My earnings were substantial, enabling my children and me to live comfortably, but I wasn't working up to the level of my ability. Goaded by this relentless voice, I induced myself to make a greater effort.

I began to read still more American, British and European financial journals and magazines, searching for ideas. Commodities continued to fascinate me, and I felt increasingly certain there would be many shortages in the years ahead. At the same time I realized that the commodities markets of South America weren't being utilized to their full potential.

My first step was to purchase sugar and various spices in Latin America, making a relatively small down payment under the terms of contracts that guaranteed annual deliveries over a period of years. This investment began to earn money from the start, and to this day continues to be profitable.

Next I studied the cement market in Europe and

North Africa, paying particular attention to developing countries that were on the verge of an industrial breakthrough. As a matter of principle I decided not to deal with any country that was ruled by a dictatorship, either of the left or the right, because that would have meant doing business with governments. Experience had taught me that whenever a government was directly involved, the bureaucratic red tape became tangled and the need to follow endless procedures was a waste of time.

That year was important to me, too, because it marked my introduction to the professional theater as an investor. I loved the theater in Madrid as an adolescent. Going to Broadway plays had been my escape and my salvation during my difficult years in New York, and I was still a theater buff. It had never occurred to me that I might form any connection with the production of either straight plays or musicals.

I had met Michael Butler on a number of occasions, a good-looking and charming man who reminded me of an English squire. I fell into conversation with him one evening at a cocktail party, and he told me he was very busy with the production of a new musical called *Hair*, which had a marvelous score. He raved so much about it that I asked if I could hear the music, and the next day he gave me a sample recording made by the composer and lyricist. Michael promised the score would "blow my mind."

I took the record home, listened to it and wasn't in the least impressed. Perhaps the poor quality of the recording was responsible, or it may be that I hadn't yet developed an appreciation of rock music. My mind wasn't blown.

About a month later Michael sent me an improved recording, along with a copy of the script. I was intrigued by the avant garde concept of the show, particularly its relevance to the troubled times in which we were living. I listened to the score in my bedroom, and as soon as I started to play the recording, my sons joined me. The boys were enthralled. It was the greatest music they had ever heard. I realized *Hair* obviously had a strong appeal for the young.

Convinced that the show had a potential, I invested in it, and even persuaded some of my friends to put money into it. I was committed.

I attended a number of rehearsals, but must admit I found it difficult to understand what was happening on the stage. The show had a message, but I was incapable of grasping it.

I was worried, too, by the nudity, and discussed this aspect of the show with Michael. He assured me the time was ripe for it, and ultimately he was proved correct. The teen-agers loved it, and so did the elderly ladies who attended matinees at the insistence of their enthusiastic grandchildren.

Preview performances were given in New York since there wasn't enough money to take the show out of town for tryouts. *Hair* was changed nightly, nobody seemed to know what was happening next, and the previews were chaotic. They were also a miserable financial failure, earning only a tiny percentage of what the show was costing. But the younger people in the audience, most of whom were given free seats, loved *Hair*, and I continued to hope for a miracle. I was relishing the whole experience and was rapidly being transformed into a true believer.

The previews went on and on, far longer than is customary for a Broadway show, but Michael was in no hurry to open. He is highly superstitious, a disciple of astrology, and I feel certain that *Hair* is the only show in Broadway history that has ever had a full-time astrologer on the payroll. Only when Countess Maria gave the word did Michael finally set an opening date.

I attended the opening with Michael's father, a well-known Chicago executive, and some of his friends. In the middle of the performance Paul Butler walked out, muttering something to the effect that another of his son's dreams had exploded. How wrong he was!

The opening night party was held at a discotheque, and everyone had fun. But Michael's absence was conspicuous. A case of opening night jitters made him ill, and he had gone home to bed. But, unable to sleep, he awaited the verdict of the newspaper critics who have the power of life and death over a show.

The reviews were better than we had expected, the show steadily gained in popularity, and soon we had a solid hit on our hands. But the early problems had created a great many debts. So I invested another substantial sum and pulled it into the black.

Success created other problems, and Michael often came to me for advice. As a rule we met late at night, sometimes as late as two in the morning. Everyone else at these meetings usually smoked pot—I have never smoked anything—and I invariably returned home with a splitting headache.

Hair was unique, setting a new trend in the theater, and I doubt there will ever be another show like it. Everyone connected with it was feverishly enthusiastic from the outset. The cast, the production people and the business staff were convinced it would become a great hit, and it did. Long lines formed daily at the box office, road companies played all over the United States and foreign productions were equally successful. *Hair* became one of the biggest moneymaking shows of all time.

As one of the principal investors I benefited handsomely. My initiation into show business had exceeded my wildest dreams, and I caught a fever from which I hope I never recover. I've gone on from being an investor to becoming an active producer in my own right, and I'm in show business to stay, not only because of the financial rewards it offers, but also because it represents a challenge. Its business methods are often haphazard and chaotic, the talented, artistic people involved are inclined to be highly temperamental, and the results, as I have sometimes learned, can be disastrous. I am convinced, however, that even the production of a play can be subjected to disciplined organization. Only time will tell whether I am right.

In the summer of 1968 I returned to Spain to see my family and look after my growing business interests. I took Carlos with me. My participation in *Hair* had been publicized, and my family heartily disapproved. People who work in the Spanish theater are not socially acceptable, and an exception is made only for the most important stars, whom it is difficult to exclude.

No one met us at the airport, a sure sign I was in the deepest disfavor, so we had to take a taxi to my parents' house. I was summoned to my father's study, and for a moment felt I was seventeen again.

My father was grim. "Get out of the theatrical business," he told me. "It's disgraceful for a member of my family to have anything to do with it. Use your time for substantial, realistic enterprises."

I didn't want to argue with my father, but I was no longer a subservient adolescent. I pointed out to him that theater people are not only accepted in the United States, but their company is eagerly sought in the highest levels. I also emphasized that I had already earned back my original investment and was anticipating very large profits.

He waved aside my facts and repeated his demands.

I became annoyed. "The money I invested is my own," I said. "I earned it, with no help from anyone. How I utilize it is my own affair."

He retreated into a cold shell, precisely as I anticipated. I spent a full month in Madrid, and not until the very last day of my visit did he speak to me on any subject other than business. The atmosphere was tense.

I went with him to his office every day, and spent most of my time learning about his various businesses. Whenever he spoke to me about the complexities of one or another of his enterprises I took notes, never interrupted and waited until he was finished before asking questions. Those questions were searching, revealing a greater understanding of his activities than he expected, and I could see that I often surprised him. But he made no comment.

On the last day of my visit, my father paid me the first compliment I could remember. "I'll be able to die in peace," he said, "because I'll be leaving my business in capable hands."

He didn't say a word about me as a person, but that would have been asking too much. At least he had developed a regard for me as an executive.

Soon after I returned to the United States it was time for the new school year to begin, and it dawned on me at long last that I no longer needed my teaching job at Columbia. I was financially secure and didn't have to reach out for a salaried position. I was still spending every morning at the school, and knew I could use that time to far better advantage.

My contract still had two years to run, however, so I felt obliged to stay. I imagine I could have gone to the authorities and obtained a release, but that was contrary to my principles. I believed in honoring every contract to the letter. My conscience wouldn't permit me to find a way out.

Until then I had thoroughly enjoyed my contacts with young people, but now my job became a chore. I continued to lecture and hold conferences with individual students, but my heart was no longer in the work. I was too preoccupied, and teaching interfered with the achievement of my still-expanding goals.

As the 1960s drew to a close many other women were beginning to enjoy the sexual freedom that had been mine for years, thanks to The Pill. I liked knowing that I had been in the vanguard.

Toward the end of the decade I became involved in another romance, but should classify it as a semi-romance. Once again, with my unerring instinct, I chose the wrong man.

He was a handsome, wealthy bachelor, who was witty and exceptionally intelligent. He reputedly went out only with the most attractive women in New York and, according to stories I heard, he was hypercritical of their appearance. I was flattered when he developed an interest in me.

I made certain to go to the beauty parlor before going out with him. I was already wearing designer clothes, but spent even more time selecting them. I was pampering myself—and enjoying it—as never before.

We attended elegant dinner parties together, went to chic restaurants and occasionally flew to Palm Beach for weekends. There we occupied adjoining bedrooms, and usually talked until the small hours of the morning. All we did, unfortunately, was talk.

I think it unlikely that he approved of my appearance. I can recall only a few times when he complimented my dress. He never, never made a pass at me, and I couldn't understand why he bothered to take me out. It was obvious he admired my mind, but that was small comfort.

I decided it was up to me to become more aggressive. When he took my arm, I stroked his arm. When our shoulders touched I leaned against him. I flirted with him as subtly as I could. Still nothing happened.

Finally, after going with him for six months, I dragged him to bed. Pure disaster. We simply didn't click.

I didn't know if the fault was mine or if he was that way with all women. Like an idiot I discussed the matter with him, and learned he had a problem, which was the reason he liked to be seen with beautiful women. For the second time I had chosen an impotent man as my lover, and I was disgusted with myself.

By this time I had learned better than to try to change a man. We had an intellectual compatibility and we enjoyed each other's company; I was content to pursue a friendship in which the element of sex was lacking. So was he and we continued to see each other, with both of us realizing that our relationship would lead to nothing more substantial. At least I had become sufficiently mature to accept my friend for what he was and not demand sex as well as companionship from him.

It occurred to me that I was growing tired of affairs for their own sake. But I realized, too, that I needed to exercise extraordinary caution before becoming romantically involved again. I simply couldn't afford to make another mistake. I even told myself the time had come for me to apply business principles to my choice of men, which was an absurd idea. Nevertheless I was learning, and I avoided serious entanglements.

In the summer of 1969 I made yet another visit to Spain. By now my parents were expecting me. I couldn't disappoint them, no matter how incapable they were of showing affection for me. I timed my trip so its end coincided with the date of the London opening of *Hair*.

I flew up to England, and learned from one of the many hippie secretaries that Michael Butler was planning to escort me to the opening. He was holding a meeting in his hotel suite, and would I join him there?

The customary confusion reigned in his suite, but I quickly discovered he had no intention of taking me to the opening. He was escorting a gorgeous English bird. Although he assured me he had put seats aside for me, no one else knew anything about these tickets, and I began to feel irritated.

Just as the whole party was about to leave for the theater, Michael discovered his shoes were missing. I assumed and still believe the hotel valet took them off to shine them, but in the uproar no one listened to me.

Crisis. Michael, who has enormous feet, had come to London only with the one pair of shoes he was wearing at the time. No other shoes would fit him.

Decision. *All* of us would go barefoot to the opening. This we did, shocking the English and accumulating a great deal of publicity.

When I had learned Michael didn't intend to take me with him I telephoned a friend, who met me at the theater. Not only was I barefoot, but I discovered my seats were in the last row. Obviously a last-minute move on the part of a staff that had forgotten to put aside tickets for one of the show's principal backers.

I was so embarrassed and annoyed that I refused to attend the cast party after the opening, and instead flew to Paris, where I had scheduled meetings with several commodities dealers. I also looked into a favorite project in which I was a minority stockholder.

A lady, Egyptian by birth, talented and charming, had commissioned Salvador Dali, one of the great artists of our day, to design a collection of magnificent table centerpieces in gold. Without much difficulty I persuaded several friends to invest. The collection should have earned a small fortune, in part because it had been designed by Dali, and partly because of the ever-increasing price of gold.

The lady who owned the majority interest proved difficult, with the result that the unfinished collection had to be placed in a vault. According to the original plans seven more pieces were to have been made, but it became increasingly difficult to find financing for them, and the majority stockholder refused to cooperate with the rest of us. To this day the superb, uncompleted collection rests in a safe deposit vault.

The failure of this venture taught me a lesson. Never again would I invest in a project unless I, or a group in which I had a dominant voice, controlled it. I still follow that practice, and have never regretted it.

Soon after I returned to New York my instinct told me I was beginning to overextend myself in South America. Some countries there were beginning to place controls on their currencies, making it more and more difficult to draw out cash. I knew I would be in serious trouble if countries froze their assets, so I pulled out while I still had the chance.

This meant I had an appreciable sum of money to invest elsewhere. I had been developing an interest in the Far East, and through a prominent Oriental lady who was a friend I obtained introductions to important businessmen in the Philippines, Thailand, India, Indonesia and Singapore. I went on an extended trip to the area to investigate the potentials.

Doing business in the Orient is an experience for which I was unprepared. Yes seldom means yes, and no is infrequently no; black is rarely black, and white is scarcely ever white. The Orient has its own tempo, its own customs, its own standards, and the Westerner who hopes to survive there, much less earn profits, is obliged to learn Oriental ways.

My first Eastern deal was a miserable failure. I learned that a bumper tobacco crop had been grown in the Philippines. The price was cheap. On the other hand, the Indonesian crop had been rained out. The price had soared. Very well, I would buy Philippine tobacco and ship it to Indonesia.

I went into partnership with a company already established in that part of the world, and at first all went well. We bought the Philippine tobacco for a reasonable sum, sent it to Indonesia and stored it in a warehouse. I was delighted when I learned we could command a price of three times what we had paid. But my partners were greedy, and insisted on waiting until we could get ten times our purchase price.

While we waited another tobacco crop ripened in Indonesia, and was enormous. The bottom dropped out of the price of tobacco, and our merchandise stayed in an old, damp warehouse that stood under a blazing tropical sun. Our tobacco spoiled, and to this day rests in that same warehouse. I was insured, of course, and also filed a lawsuit to cover at least the cost of my original investment, but the case is complicated and still hasn't been settled in court.

Finding myself in a produce-or-perish situation, I quickly learned how to do business in the Far East. Because I had no alternative, I soon made a number of sound investments there. The Orient has been good to me—in more ways than one. Back in New York, after one of my trips to the East, I met two Oriental ladies who wanted to form a new shipping company. When I expressed an interest in the venture they invited me to dine with them and the president of a New York shipping company who also saw the potential of the idea.

The ladies refused to eat Western food. We met at a

Chinese restaurant of their choice. About ten of us were seated around a large table. The president of the shipping company, who proved to be ruggedly handsome and surprisingly young, sat on the far side of the table from me. I had no chance to exchange a word with him, principally because he was smothered by the two Oriental ladies, who flanked him. He was "their" shipping company president, and they intended to allow no one else to get near him.

He was aware of my existence, however, and I accepted when he offered to drive me home. As I recall it, we had a pleasant chat, confining our conversation to business matters. The deal never materialized.

Our paths didn't cross again for a number of months. I made yet another trip to the East, and became involved in a complicated deal requiring the services of a shipping company that—using Indonesia as a base—would carry merchandise to and from India and Japan. I applied for a license, but because I was unfamiliar with shipping, I needed a partner who knew that business.

I remembered the man I'd met at the New York restaurant; he was a member of my own generation, and from the little I'd seen of him he had seemed to know his business. I wrote to him. He sent one of his executives to meet me and we discussed the plans in some detail.

Several months passed, and I was again making a visit to Djakarta. While there, I was informed that my shipping license would be issued. I cabled the shipping company president, and his office forwarded my message to him in Japan, where he had gone on a business trip.

He cabled me from Tokyo, saying he would join me for a meeting in Indonesia the following day.

The very name of Djakarta is romantic, especially to people who have never been there. It combines the primitive—scarcely out of the Stone Age—with the modern industrial-military, and it has an overlay of Dutch culture. Located in the heart of the tropics, it is hot, humid, stifling and filthy. Its new office buildings are as impersonal as those in other great cities. Its slums are among the most extensive in the world, and at the beginning of the 1970's many hundreds of thousands slept in the streets. Plants grow as one watches them, and even the frogs are enormous.

In this confused, bustling place with its sharp contrasts and unromantic atmosphere, I had my second meeting with Peter Holzer.

I went to a beauty parlor before he arrived and overdressed for the evening. Not that I had any personal interest in him. No, indeed. But he would be the first Westerner I'd met in some time.

Peter's flight from Tokyo had been long and tedious, but he insisted on taking me to dinner. My protests were feeble, and for the first time in fifteen years I broke my self-imposed rule and flirted with a business associate.

That night our joint business venture was the sole topic of our conversation, and though we discussed it in detail, Peter was attentive to me, which was more than he had been during our previous meeting in New York.

The next morning we had breakfast together. Followed by lunch. Followed by dinner, then dancing under the stars. Followed by talk and more talk—on subjects far removed from business—that lasted until dawn. Followed by another breakfast, another lunch and another dinner.

To say that I flipped is an understatement. Peter was intelligent, strong, fun to be with, and roughly my own age. He was ethical. Witty. Jovial on occasion. Good-looking. *And* he was a bachelor.

He was straightforward, direct, uncomplicated. He was as interested in me—my life, my thinking, my desires, my ambitions—as I was in him. He had a firm, no nonsense approach to business, in which he was successful, and he applied these same principles to his personal life.

We spent eight days together, and by the time Peter returned to the United States I knew This Was It. Good-bye, father image. Good-bye, romances with neurotics. Hello, love.

I quickly abandoned my high-flown plan never to marry again. I had no intention of letting Peter get away. Never would I encounter anyone even remotely like him. He hadn't yet asked me to marry him, but I knew he would. There had been no doubt about it from the time of our first dinner together, even though I'm sure he didn't realize it then.

When he left Djakarta I casually gave him some toys and games to deliver to my children for me. This meant that by the time I returned to New York a short time later, Peter and my sons would already be getting acquainted.

Two months after I came home we decided to marry. And we did, without delay.

I'd be guilty of gross exaggeration if I claimed that

our life together was made up of moonlight and roses from the very start. Both of us were adults, with our own habits, likes and dislikes, and lifestyles. Both of us had to adjust, and that meant hard work.

Peter had never lived with children, and overnight found himself the stepfather of two noisy, growing boys. I wanted to arrange everything on both sides, to smooth paths and help, but I had the good sense to mind my own business. Peter and the boys worked out their relations in their own, masculine way, without interference from me.

First came respect, then affection. Today Peter regards the boys as *his* sons, and they think of him as *their* father. My worries were groundless, and not long ago, when I told them how happy I am that their relationship has worked out so well, all three of them laughed at me. "What made you imagine it wouldn't?" they asked, and for once I was delighted to be patronized by males.

Peter and I had to make major adjustments in our relations with each other. I had been reared in a culture-conscious European family, and he was an all-American male. I loved ballet, and he hated it. Nothing can tear him away from a football game, and nothing can persuade me to watch one.

We realized we had to work out a *modus vivendi* based on compromise. Sometimes we would go to a detective or thriller movie, sometimes to a more intellectual film. I found the whodunits weren't as atrocious as I'd imagined, and he discovered he enjoyed the more esoteric movies.

I couldn't become interested in football, baseball or basketball. My mind wandered, and I was bored. I tried, but I failed, so again we compromised. I stayed home, reading or working, while Peter and the boys happily trooped off together to a game.

I was afraid that problems caused by my vocational life would be more difficult to adjust, and before we were married I laid my cards on the table. As he knew, I had struggled to create my business life, I had been successful, and I had no intention of giving up my career. I would respect him, and I expected him to respect me.

I would continue to operate my business in my own way, just as he would run his own operations without interference from me. It was a relief to hear him say he had never contemplated any other approach.

As things have worked out, we know a great deal about each other's businesses. We have developed a true partnership, and I can't begin to count the evenings we have spent exchanging ideas and opinions, seeking each other's advice and heeding each other's judgments.

I am proud of Peter's accomplishments, and he is proud of mine. Both of us have taken care to insure that no pettiness has ever entered into our business discussions. This, too, has taken work, but the results have been worth it. When one of us triumphs, we're both proud and happy. When one of us fails, both of us are miserable.

For a long time we went our separate ways in business, each taking care not to step on the other's feet. Our partnership in every other phase of life has been so successful that recently we have gone into several ventures jointly. These efforts have been successful because we have simply extended our partnership. Neither of us is president and the other vice-president. I respect Peter's areas of expertise, he respects mine, and together we made quite a team.

All the torments of earlier personal relations were a necessary preparation for my present, completely contented existence, which I couldn't have achieved without making mistakes and learning from them. How extraordinary—and how wonderful—it is to have real peace of mind!

Twelve

My investment in *Hair* made me a natural target for every Broadway producer who sought financing, but I avoided commitments in spite of my eagerness to have another fling in the theater. I wanted to wait until I found something that really aroused my enthusiasm, and I had a secret desire to become a producer myself. Only Peter knew of this ambition; I was too shy to mention it to anyone else because, after all, I lacked experience in the medium.

One day I heard about *Where Has Tommy Flowers Gone?* a new play by Terrence McNally. I had liked his last play, and when I learned I could see *Tommy Flowers* at the Berkshire festival I hurried up to see it. I loved it.

I called the producer and told him I would take care of the bulk of the financing provided he made me a co-producer. He agreed, and we had a deal.

It didn't take long for me to discover that my title was empty. The producer played on my naïvete and my eagerness to be a part of the theater. He would handle the bookings, as I knew nothing about that aspect of the business. He would order the sets, costumes and props because I was too busy a lady for such matters, and besides, he knew I wouldn't want to get involved with carpenters, stagehands and other workers.

I was quietly indignant. It hadn't been all that long since I had been a "worker" myself. I could talk the language of laborers, I admired their outspoken attitudes and I wasn't afraid of getting dirt on my Gucci shoes. I was being manipulated, but I was such a neophyte that I kept my mouth shut.

The producer calmly worked around me. With the author's blessing he chose the director, and together they cast the play. It was apparent to me that the actress hired as the leading lady was suffering from emotional problems that would create difficulties, but no one listened to me when I mentioned it. Unfortunately my observation became a reality and she had a complete breakdown and had to be replaced—to the detriment of the play.

Never having studied playwriting I had to rely on my instincts, and felt too insecure to express my thoughts about faults in the play that seemed plain to me. I made extensive notes, however, and after the openings I compared them with the comments of the critics. We agreed, so perhaps I wasn't as much of a greenhorn as I had thought.

The play lasted eight weeks on Broadway, and suffered financial losses. I made up all of the deficit, as the producer never paid his share. I promised myself that the next time I became involved with a play I would apply the principles that governed my other business enterprises. I would be in the driver's seat.

I hadn't lost my appetite for the theater because I had been burned, and I was determined not to repeat my mistakes. But other matters intervened for a number of months. Show business had to take a back seat.

My husband and I went to Europe, each of us to attend to his own business deals. While I was in Paris, I had a telephone call from my father, asking if I could come to Madrid without delay as he needed my help. Imagine! My *father* actually *needed* me!

I flew to Madrid and learned that my father couldn't fulfill a contract to supply cement to Syria as the plant he owned wasn't producing as much as he needed for the purpose. I learned the basic principle of living up to contracts from him, and he was frantic.

As it happened I was able to handle the problem without difficulty for him, and I'm sure I showed off a bit for his benefit. I simply telephoned the owner of a cement plant in Italy, a man with whom I had done business in the past, and arranged for him to make the cement delivery. As frosting on the cake I received a commission for the freight charges, but the sweetest dividend of all was the admiration I saw in my father's eyes.

After Peter and I returned home from Europe I began reading plays again, many plays, but I soon discovered each of them had a producer. I decided I would wait until the opportune time.

Meanwhile I had more than enough to keep me occupied. My contract with Columbia University expired, and I finally left. I had more time for my husband and children, and more flexibility when it was necessary for me to travel.

I bought more sugar, rice and spices, leasing sound

warehouses abroad to hold them until prices rose higher. I knew I was speculating, and I even sold some real estate properties so I'd have more cash for this purpose. I was convinced that commodity prices would soar and that the time for a rise was approaching rapidly. So I wanted to be in a position to earn extensive profits when that time came.

I became more involved in my father's business affairs, and at about this time he gave me the task of straightening out a deteriorating situation in an America-based tool manufacturing company. He was the principal stockholder and gave me free rein to do whatever I thought necessary.

A preliminary survey indicated that a number of the company's officials were elderly and that their approach to business was old-fashioned. The president, however, posed a different problem. It took a great deal of digging for me to discover that he operated out of an expensive suite of offices, enjoyed bear hunting in Alaska by helicopter and had a predilection for French mistresses. His private life was his own, to be sure, but he was charging his expenses for his various pleasures to the company.

It was impossible to discharge him outright as he still had several years to run on an ironclad ten-year contract my father had given him. I discussed the matter with an official of the bank that was a small partner, and he agreed that we'd have a lawsuit on our hands if I simply discharged the president.

So I tried another approach. Some delicate snooping on my part revealed that the president sometimes entertained girls in his office after business hours. That was all I needed to know, and I started dropping in at his office around six in the evening. Sure enough, one evening I caught him presiding at an orgy, and he was deeply embarrassed.

I wasted no time, and asked the chairman of the board to call an emergency directors' meeting while the president was still suffering from the shock of exposure. The meeting was held the very next day.

Only the bank officer, who was also a director of the company, knew what I had in mind. I began questioning the president about his travel expenses; I was very precise and deliberately tormented him. The bank officer joined in the questioning, and soon we had the president cornered. The following morning he resigned.

As he had caused us less trouble than I had anticipated, I suggested giving him a substantial payment in return for a written release from all contractural obligations. I always like to take precautions, and sometimes I'm inclined to be overly careful, but I believe this attitude pays off.

With the president out of the way I took over the difficult task of reorganizing a corporation whose executives were set in their ways. I held a private talk with each senior employee, encouraging each to be frank, and asked each to give me a written statement outlining his areas of responsibility and his suggestions for improvements in production, management and sales.

After three days of conferences I began to see daylight. Several men who were earning large salaries had created their own little power empires, padding their payrolls with superfluous employees in order to build up their own importance. I discharged them, redistributed responsibilities and thus won the confidence and support of the other executives. I made most of the promotions from inside the corporation, which further encouraged them, and I became active in bringing in several new accounts.

Throughout this entire operation I knew I was walking on eggs. I was resented because I was an outsider, because I was my father's representative and, above all, because I was a woman. I am convinced that in almost any business situation a woman must display more tact, delicacy and finesse than a man. Had I barged in swinging an ax, as a man might have done, they would have closed ranks against me, and their hostile opposition would have made my task far more difficult.

On the other hand, I believe, a woman has some natural advantages in business, and is foolish if she doesn't utilize them. In this situation I was sympathetic. I listened. I encouraged confidences. Without going so far as to take the "helpless female" approach, I nevertheless made it plain that I was relying on the company's executives for the solution of our mutual problems. The direct result was that most of them gave me their enthusiastic cooperation. The more efficient and secure the man, in my experience, the more forthright and candid his response to a challenge.

The tool company was on its feet again. It was slightly disconcerting to discover that my father wasn't in the least surprised, having taken it for granted that I'd be successful. I enjoyed the compliment.

While I was catching my breath I learned that Galt McDermott and Gerry Ragni, the composer and lyricist, respectively, of *Hair*, had written a new musical they wanted me to hear. Gerry had also written the "book," as the libretto of today's musical is called. We met. Galt played the tunes on the piano and I was impressed by the music. It was terrific. The lyrics were amusing and bright. I asked to read the script.

Gerry reached into an oversized, hippie-type bag and hauled out a bulky mess of about two thousand pages.

"Wow!" I exclaimed as I reached for the pile. "You've written a Bible."

He drew back in alarm. "You can't see it!"

I had learned something about sensitive artists, and I knew Gerry. "I can't possibly produce a play I haven't seen," I said. "I'd very much like to read the book."

He began to pace up and down. "Why the hell are you calling my writing a book?" he demanded.

Other people, it seemed, wrote the books of musical plays, but that was old-fashioned. What Gerry had done, no more and no less, was his "writing."

Very well. I insisted on the right to read his writing, or I wouldn't be able to make judgments.

Finally I persuaded him to let me see the bundle, and I tried to plow through it. I am capable of reading, writing and understanding the English language, but I couldn't make sense out of what Gerry had written. He had fresh, sparkling ideas, however, and occasionally I detected a glimmer of what he was attempting to say.

I decided to go ahead with the new show, which was called *Dude*. As I saw it, we would hire a director. Then Gerry and the director would lock themselves into a room somewhere and reduce the chaotic mess of a book to something orderly. We would see the beginning of a story line from which we would, as our next step, spin the plot that critics and audiences demand.

As we began to organize the show I couldn't help

hoping that a blast of wind would scatter those thousands of pages of intermittent brilliance while Gerry was climbing in or out of a taxi, taking a subway or stopping for a drink in one of the crummy bars he favored. No such luck.

In fact, the mess was becoming messier. Every night Gerry enjoyed vivid, significant dreams, and the following morning he tried to incorporate them into his libretto, churning out more pages. I continued to rely on the director we hired to straighten out the situation.

Meanwhile my husband joined me as the co-producer of *Dude*. My enthusiasm for the project was contagious, so he followed my example, invested a large sum in the show and became active in raising the rest of the money necessary for the production.

We were not producers in the usual sense of the word. Rather we were psychologists, headshrinkers, handholders, beggars and actors. There were days when I thought we were better actors, necessarily, than the people we would hire to appear onstage.

Logic is a feeble weapon when dealing with intense, creative people, and Gerry rarely bothered to listen to reason. So we hit on a technique of acting out the various problems that arose. Sometimes we actually managed to convince him of the validity of the goals we were trying to achieve.

One of our principal problems arose during the early days of production. Gerry demanded a stage filled with dirt. Real dirt. Our misgivings quickly were justified: Dirt would choke the actors and spread a film of dust over the entire theater, including an unappreciative audience. Gerry couldn't see the problem our way, so one day we literally rolled in the dirt for him, choking and being forced to spit it out repeatedly. That convinced him, and he was willing to abandon the idea.

Mounting this musical required extraordinary skills and even more patience. Negotiations with everyone connected with the show were protracted and complicated. Furthermore, we were required to negotiate a highly unusual contract with the owners of the theater that permitted us to transform the orchestra pit, making it part of the stage. This drastically increased our budget. We had to raise the staggering sum of seven hundred and fifty thousand dollars. Fortunately, we were able to persuade a major record company to make a substantial investment.

The book was far too long when we began to play previews, and as soon as we placed the show before audiences we realized that more than major cuts in the libretto were needed. The director was completely dominated by the author, and consequently was incapable of performing the major surgery that was needed. So we changed directors, hiring the one man we believed able to reduce the work to a size and shape that could be staged effectively.

This shift, which caused changes in sets, costume and lighting, punched huge holes in our budget, but ultimately resulted in a much-improved show. We were confident we were at last on the right track.

Alas, in spite of a spectacular score that was enthusiastically received by audiences, the show failed to take off. The critics disliked it. The existentialist theme was difficult for many people to understand, although those who did were enthusiastic. We reconciled ourselves to failure and closed *Dude,* with all the work and dedication, not to say a very large sum of money, going down the drain.

Peter and I were shattered by the nightmare and went on our boat for a cruise. The ocean was calm, and by the time we reached Florida we were able to think clearly again. There is little as devastating as a failure of such proportions, and we made a joint, serious effort to analyze our errors.

We had not been wrong, we decided, to engage in the project in the first place. It was exciting, with a truly first-rate score, and had it succeeded it would have been a major force in the transformation of the musical theater.

Our biggest mistake had been to go into production before the script was in relatively final shape. Also, we should have taken far greater care to insure, with the assistance of our managers and other professional theater people, that the production would remain within our budget. In addition, when we had realized that *Dude* had few commercial possibilities we should have put sentiment aside, dropped it and cut our losses.

Show business, as I was continuing to learn, was unlike any other. Its lifeblood is emotion, and the attachments that are formed become all-encompassing. One laughs and cries with the author. One forms close ties with the director, the scenic designer, the costumer, the choreographer. One joins the actors and actresses in a very private, exclusive club. When these ties are shattered, rudely and abruptly, one feels as though a close relative has died.

The impact on me was still stronger. I had unwittingly pulled my husband into the venture with me, and to make matters still worse, it was the first time we had ever gone into an enterprise together. My guilt was overwhelming, and it made me feel no better when he refused to blame me.

We soon agreed that, for the present, neither of us would have anything more to do with show business. Peter hadn't enjoyed the publicity, which had contributed nothing to his business image, and had particularly disliked being regarded as a Broadway playboy. He is an earnest, dedicated businessman, and it was ludicrous to think of him in any other way.

The failure did no harm to our marriage. Each of us quickly realized we had our own fields of expertise, and decided to concentrate on what we knew. As a result of the nightmare we drew still closer.

The collapse of *Dude* was beneficial, too, in my relations with my children. Both boys are sensitive and were stunned by the bad publicity we received and we grew closer.

I try to face a crisis with my eyes open and had a long, frank talk with my sons. I made no attempt to whitewash myself or justify my mistakes. I had stupidly developed an oversized ego, and now I had been hauled down to earth with a painful thump, which had been good for me.

I emphasized to the boys that they had entertained too high an opinion of me. Out of vanity I had encouraged that regard.

The boys were loyal, and tried to argue with me, but I refused to listen. I pointed out my errors, painful mistake by painful mistake. I stressed that I was too emotional for my own good and too inclined to blame circumstances when my own judgment was poor.

I realize I was scourging myself, getting rid of my guilts by forcing them to recognize the fact that their mother was as fallible as anyone else. But the talk was good for them. Until my marriage to Peter I had offered them the only security they had ever known, and my failure was an emotional cathartic that helped them readjust their own values. With the collapse of *Dude,* their mother was no longer someone who could do no wrong, and they adopted a healthier attitude that would enable them to face the world more realistically. When seen in that perspective, the cost of my mishap had not been too high.

Thirteen

By the time we returned from Florida I knew that ultimately I would return to show business, but in the right way. I would utilize the principles I had learned in other businesses, and I would curb the excesses of artistic temperaments rather than be controlled by them. I would judge a play by its commercial potential and would produce it only if the author and director could respond favorably to the pressures induced by the need to make changes that would create a success.

So much for the theater. I had to make up for lost time and lost income.

I flew to many places, buying and storing commodities. Because of increasing inflation I sold my stocks and got out of the market. By this time I owned a cooperative apartment building, but I was afraid a financial recession was coming, which would mean that people would be unwilling and unable to pay ever-increasing maintenance costs. I sold the building just in time to earn a handsome profit. After six months of hard work I knew I was not stagnating, and my guilt eased somewhat.

My husband is a man who wants and needs physical exercise. Spending all of our time in New York made him restless. He suggested we buy a place in the country for weekends and summers. I had become so acclimated to city living that his suggestion startled me, but I knew he was right, for the sake of the boys and our own sakes.

We launched an intensive search, and soon found an attractive house in New Jersey, surrounded by ample acreage, in which we invested. That house represented our one stroke of good fortune; over the next few months we were stricken by a series of personal disasters.

A dear friend dropped dead one weekend when we went on a skiing trip with him and his wife.

Our boat was shipwrecked on the rocks near Newport, Rhode Island, when the captain fell asleep at the wheel.

The explosion of a gas line in the basement virtually demolished our town house while we were on a business trip to the Orient.

The destruction of our house was a tragedy so great that I can scarcely describe it. That house was my *home,* an extension of myself. It wasn't a rented apartment, it wasn't a cooperative apartment. It was a real home, the symbol of my roots in America, my marriage, my complete family life. It was an integral part of me, and I had poured my soul into its decoration.

The basement, the kitchen area and the library above the kitchen had been transformed into piles of rubble. Heat, light and water were unavailable. Our beautiful antiques and rugs, furniture and paintings and bric-a-brac that had survived the explosion at the rear of the house were exposed to the elements in midwinter.

We had to move into a hotel, which made me desperately unhappy, and months passed before repair work was even started. The procrastination of our insurance company drove me almost out of my mind. They wanted to rebuild with the cheapest materials available, and I wouldn't stand for it. They haggled over the price of the antiques and other valuables that had been destroyed. It was obvious to me that they were simply trying to wear us down.

A home isn't as important to a man as it is to a woman, and for the sake of peace my husband would have settled with the insurance company. I refused. No insurance company was going to push me around. I hate lawsuits of any kind and had never sued anyone in my life, but that didn't stop me. I decided we would do our own rebuilding, then sue the insurance company for the difference between their settlement offer and the actual cost.

This is what we did, and the uproar was so unsettling I found it difficult to concentrate. I couldn't give any of the parties at which I transacted so much of my business. I was deprived of my office, and could hold no meetings at home.

In the midst of all this chaos my attention was called to a new play, *Brain*, which I saw in Boston. It concerned the problems of being a woman, and I not only went wild over it, but thought it could be transformed into a marvelous musical. I persuaded Galt MacDermott and Hal David to write the music and lyrics, respectively.

Two months later Galt quit, deciding he didn't want to do another show so soon after writing *Dude* and *Via*

Gallactica. That left me with the choice of either abandoning the venture or finding a composer whose talents were equal to those of Hal David as a lyricist. I chose the latter course, and enticed Michel LeGrand into coming to New York from Paris for a weekend to see a run-through. He liked the show, joined Hal for his first Broadway enterprise and together they wrote a beautiful score.

Problems developed during rehearsals, but when I pointed out faults the author/director rebelled. Under the terms of Dramatist Guild contracts, no word of a play can be changed without the author's permission, and he has the final word on casting. If he proves unreasonable, a producer may either drop the whole venture or give in. I elected to allow myself to be persuaded that all would be well.

By the last week of rehearsals I was miserable. Only my husband knew it, as it was imperative that the company's morale not be destroyed. We went to Philadelphia for the opening, and I knew disaster was impending. I was right.

The dress rehearsal was horrendous. The dancers couldn't work on the slanted floor. The choreography was amateurish, the costumes were pretentious. The sets were rigid and unworkable, some of the singers couldn't act and several of the actors couldn't sing. All the flaws I'd seen at rehearsals were enlarged, and still others developed that I hadn't anticipated.

I returned to our hotel and paced our suite all night. Peter tried without success to calm me down. Arnim, who had come with us, did his best to placate me, but I wouldn't listen.

The opening night reviews were merciless. The author proved incapable of making revisions. I brought several prominent directors to Philadelphia, among them Michael Kidd, Frank Corsaro and Mel Shapiro, but all of them regarded the show as hopeless and refused to touch it. I cut our losses by closing in Philadelphia.

Once again I had been burned by allowing myself to be double-talked into believing all would be well. I shouldn't have allowed the author to direct the show herself as the performance of both functions by one person destroys perspective. Only such theatrical geniuses as George S. Kaufman and Noel Coward have been capable of directing their own plays.

I should have taken a firmer stand during rehearsals, and if the author had remained recalcitrant I should have terminated my association with the production then and there.

The emotional crisis I suffered was far less severe than my trauma after the failure of *Dude*. This time I knew I would return to show business again, and I promised myself that things would be different. Never again would I allow my own judgment to be overruled.

Certainly my business judgment was vindicated when, a short time later, the commodities markets rose sharply. I began to sell the sugar, rice, spices and other commodities I had been accumulating for several years. I earned a great deal of money. Had I chosen to wait until prices soared even higher I could have made still more, but I had already taken enough of a risk and was satisfied. It doesn't pay to be greedy.

In the spring of 1973, Terrence McNally came to me

with two one-act plays, which he lumped together under a single title, *Bad Habits.* I thought the plays were riotously funny, and knowing that Terrence could rewrite if it became necessary, I produced *Bad Habits* Off Broadway.

I felt no need to intervene during rehearsals, which went smoothly, and we opened to rave reviews. In three months the cost was paid off.

I decided to move the play to a Broadway theater, even though it was late in the season. The cost of the move was exorbitant, and although the play had a respectable run it couldn't make up those costs, so I closed it.

The following year I became involved with another play by Terrence McNally, initially called *The Tubs.* I first saw it in New Haven at the Yale Repertory Theatre, and liked it, although it wasn't yet ready for a New York audience. I suggested to Terrence that he make it less crude for Broadway, while at the same time strengthening both the plot and the humor.

He agreed and went back to work. By September 1974, he returned with a much improved play, under a new name, *The Ritz.* I was delighted, and agreed to produce it. We cast three well-known players in the leading roles and were ready to go into rehearsals at the end of October.

One evening while we were making our last, prerehearsal preparations, my telephone rang.

"I'm Dustin Hoffman," the man at the other end of the line said.

"I'm the Queen of Greece," I replied.

Well, it really was Dustin Hoffman calling. He

wanted me to read a new play by Murray Schisgal and, if I liked it, to discuss it with me. Speed was essential, he said, and promised to explain when he saw me.

That same night I received a copy of the play, *All Over Town,* and liked it.

The next morning Dustin and Murray appeared at my house. The play would mark Dustin's debut as a director. The cast had been hired and the set designed, but the producer had just backed out. Unless another producer stepped into the breach within the next seventy-two hours the cast would be forced to disband.

I read the play again, and yet again. Dustin explained his production and staging ideas, and although he had never before directed a play, his ideas were sound. And thoroughly professional.

All through our long conversations Murray Schisgal just sat, not saying a word. Later I found him to be a witty, highly intelligent and charming man, but during these talks he looked bored and sullen. After having the production of his play canceled on the eve of rehearsals I couldn't blame him for being skeptical.

I agreed to produce the play, made the contacts necessary to raise money and met with immediate success. Dustin promised to raise money too, and did. Within forty-eight hours we were in business.

Suddenly I was producing two plays simultaneously. The *All Over Town* company was in Washington, and stayed there. *The Ritz* rehearsed in New York prior to its pre-Broadway opening in Washington. I tried to be in two places at the same time, and almost succeeded.

I was reminded of the early 1960s, when I had worked from early morning until late at night. I missed meals and forgot sleep. My husband and sons were marvelously patient when I seemed to forget they existed.

I tried to divide my time equally between the two companies because artistic people are inclined to be jealous, and I didn't want word to get out over the actors' grapevine that I favored one over the other. That not only would have hurt morale, but might have persuaded sensitive people that I regarded *their* play as a potential failure. Which I didn't.

Watching Dustin Hoffman direct a rehearsal was a thrill. He is the most thorough director I've ever seen, paying attention to infinite details. His patience is unending, his sense of timing is superb, and he dedicates every waking moment to his work. I learned a great deal from him, and I cherish every moment of those rehearsals.

All Over Town got off to a slow start. The Washington reviews were bad, and two members of the cast were weak. But I wasn't really worried. The play was amusing, Murray was amenable to suggestions and little by little the company improved. I knew Dustin would recognize the weakness of the two actors who weren't as good as the rest of the cast. I refrained from interfering and eventually he replaced them.

We opened to fairly good reviews in New York. Clive Barnes, of the *New York Times,* whose opinion counted most, liked the show very much. So did the audiences, and *All Over Town* was a hit.

Meanwhile *The Ritz* was in trouble. One of the actors obviously was miscast, but the director and author balked when I wanted him replaced. This time I put my foot down hard, and in the second week of rehearsals a new actor was hired for the role.

The play itself was confusing in spots. Although I had an understanding with Terrence, he didn't seem to agree with me and did very little rewriting.

Washington would provide the test. If the reviews were good, I knew, Terrence wouldn't listen to me, and the play would be a failure in New York. Only if the critics disliked *The Ritz* would he listen to reason.

When I first saw the set on the stage of the National Theatre I was horrified. It was painted gray and looked like a battleship. I put on a temperamental scene of my own, and was so upset that no one quarreled with me. The set was repainted red before the opening.

Bobby Drivas, the director, performed a last-minute miracle by transforming three acts into two just before the opening, and this change helped. But the reviews were bad, nevertheless, as the critics pointed out the play's weaknesses and confusions.

The next day I got together with Terrence and Bobby, and laid down the law, telling them precisely what I wanted done to improve the play. Terrence balked.

I told him he was privileged to accept the changes or reject them, as he saw fit. But there was no law that compelled me to produce a play I knew would be a failure. If he refused to make the changes, I would close the play.

Terrence gave in to a brief fit of artistic temperament, then locked himself in his hotel room and went to work.

I returned to Acapulco—where I was vacationing—in order to give him and Bobby time to work out the problems. When I returned to Washington *The Ritz* was a vastly improved play. Terrence proved he was a real professional by continuing to polish lines and situations, and Bobby demonstrated his skills as a director with deft touches. I believe both are very talented.

The Ritz opened in New York to excellent reviews, some of them raves, and the audiences loved the play. Hit number two.

I was also involved in a third Broadway show, *Sherlock Holmes,* as a co-producer. This play had been done in London, where it was a great success. The cast was perfect and the direction brilliant. I had very little to do. Hit number three.

In January, 1975, I found myself with three simultaneous successes on my hands. This is a record for a woman producer. I was satisfied that I had met the challenge of show business.

But my head never got too big for my hat. I am highly sensitive to the fact that, in spite of every precaution, a new play is always a potential disaster. There is no more speculative business than the theater.

As I write these lines I have been able to add another success to my string. I'm proud of my production of Scott Joplin's only opera, *Treemonisha,* which was an artistic and commercial success in the autumn of 1975, and was hailed as one of the most important musical events of the decade. Hit number four. Now I'm producing *Monsters*—an Off Broadway play, which opened to raving reviews.

I'm sure it helps to be stagestruck, but as I look back at my experiences during the production of *Hair,* I wonder how I survived.

Tom O'Horgan, the director, opened each day's rehearsal with what he called "sensitivity exercises." One of his favorites was that of having all twenty-three actors and actresses in the company form a circle, close their eyes and stiffen their backs. Those who stood around the circle could lean against others if they felt dizzy, but the actor in the center was in danger of falling flat on his face.

The theme of *Hair* consisted of two magic words, "hang loose," which meant that everyone was expected to do precisely what he wanted. One of Michael Butler's secretaries urged me to throw out all of my designer clothes and insisted on escorting me to several Greenwich Village boutiques. I actually bought a few dresses that vaguely resembled pillowcases, and wore them when I was with the *Hair* people so I wouldn't look too unlike them.

But I drew the line when Michael went on an Indian kick and tried to persuade me to wear a ribbon around my forehead. Even with a full headdress I wouldn't even vaguely resemble an American Indian.

During this phase Michael conceived the idea that everyone connected with *Hair* was a member of a tribe. Three words were in constant use: peace, love and tribe. Michael delivered daily lectures on the subject, and Tom proposed that everyone actually live in the theater. This idea, fortunately, proved impractical.

As a matter of fact, the show was in its second week of rehearsals when I discovered, to my astonishment, that it didn't yet have a home. The management of the Biltmore Theatre was finally persuaded to allow the show to be presented there to fill an interim booking. It ran, as they say, forever.

The concept of nudity, which became a hallmark of

Hair, was introduced only a week before the opening, when some members of the cast were persuaded to strip onstage. Stripping was an important part of the hippie culture, according to Michael.

The night of the first preview was a real shocker when, at the end of the first act, three male members of the cast appeared in the nude. Members of the company supposedly were allowed to disrobe or stay dressed, as they pleased, but Michael was disappointed and threatened to bring in some outsiders who would be willing to appear naked. That turned the tide, and other members of the company began to strip, too.

In the furor that followed I sometimes wondered how I, a product of one of the most puritanical countries on earth, had become involved in such a production. To tell the truth, I didn't know what I was doing, and originally thought I had merely invested in a very liberal musical.

Before the first preview I asked several members of the cast if they knew what the show was all about, and they had to admit they didn't. During the almost seven weeks of previews the same performance was never given twice, and small wonder. Considering the fact that Gerry Ragni was one of the authors, almost anything was likely to happen. One night an actor dressed as a gorilla roared down the aisle and onto the stage on a motorcycle, but this experiment was too dangerous to be repeated.

When I produced *Where Has Tommy Flowers Gone?* I made the mistake of having the opening night party at our house. We expected seventy-five guests, but everyone feels privileged to bring family, friends and lover-of-the-moment, so more than two hundred turned up. Our delicately furnished brownstone was filled, wall to wall, with people drinking and smoking. The coughing, dizzy hostess was spaced-out on the fumes.

Another opening I recall vividly was that of a play called, *Charlie Was Here and Gone,* in which I invested but had no hand in the production. The opening night party was held in a small restaurant, and before it broke up I asked the manager of the show, his wife and another couple to join us at home for a nightcap.

My husband and I had barely arrived home when the doorbell rang. The maid opened the door, and from the living room landing on the second floor I could see a huge mob pouring into the house. Instead of four guests we had a hundred and fifty to two hundred, with everyone connected with the show and members of their entourages showing up.

The problem was that we were almost out of liquor. We had nothing in the house but several cases of magnificent Dom Perignon champagne that Joan Crawford had sent us. Our butler asked if he could serve some, and before we knew what was happening all of the precious champagne had vanished. I doubt if one person in ten knew what he was drinking.

Joan Crawford was one of the most charming show business people I've ever met. Until the day of her death she enjoyed enormous popularity, even though she retired years ago after marrying the head of Pepsi-Cola.

I don't think I'll ever forget a trip I made with her in a private Pepsi-Cola airplane to attend some motorcar races in the Midwest. She was to deliver a short speech and present the prizes that Pepsi was offering to the winners.

We went through the usual celebrity routines that, I assumed, had become routine in her life. Newspaper reporters and television crews were on hand to greet her at the airport. Motorcycle policemen escorted us to and from the races.

What I didn't realize was that Joan Crawford, in spite of her long exposure to the public, became nervous—just like the rest of us—when she was forced to confront a large crowd. Well, on this occasion she made a splendid little address, speaking mostly about Pepsi and holding a frosted glass bearing the Pepsi logo, from which she sipped from time to time. What her audience didn't know was the glass contained gin, which helped see her through the ordeal.

Her informality was wonderful, especially to someone like me, who was brought up in such a strict, proper atmosphere. One night Joan and I went to a very posh French restaurant for dinner. We were bowed to our table, and the whole staff made a huge fuss over her. While she was having her cocktail, and with a half-dozen waiters still hovering nearby, Joan suddenly noticed that her huge diamond solitaire was smudged. Not caring what anyone thought, she slipped it off her finger and washed it in gin!

She and many other show business friends have been good for me. If I've contributed anything to show business, as I hope I have, they've done a great deal for me. So many people I've met in the theater are warm and generous.

It is difficult to see ourselves as others see us, but I'm

sure I was too formal, too rigidly polite before I became involved in the theater. Certainly show business people have hastened and completed the process of my Americanization. I'm grateful, and can't ask for more than that.

Fourteen

While writing this book it occurred to me that I've enjoyed certain privileges denied to most people. I've traveled to every continent, I'm well acquainted with most of the world's major cities. I know many out of the way places. I've spent long enough periods in various places to have become thoroughly familiar with the customs and attitudes of many lands.

Not until recent years, after my marriage to Peter, did I think in terms of traveling for pleasure. Travel, to me, was a business necessity, and my business took me to many places. Only as I look back over the miles and years do I realize how fortunate I've been.

Some of my most unusual experiences took place during several long visits to Indonesia. On one trip, I was invited to a Chinese wedding and knew only that Indonesians of Chinese descent still abide by ancient customs. The parents of the bride were moderately wealthy and could afford the best for their daughter, and I was curious.

The day of the wedding was a sizzler, with the temperature standing above 115 degrees Fahrenheit, and the humidity very high, too. The fourteen-year-old bride wore a floor-length, long-sleeved dress of pink wool, as well as white gloves, and the twenty-two-year-old bridegroom also was encased in wool.

All of the guests seemed to arrive at the same time, and stood patiently outside the front door of the house. I was the only Caucasian present. When everyone had assembled we were shown into what appeared to be a drawing room. There were approximately sixty of us, and we stood in total silence, staring at each other. I found myself becoming acutely bored.

Then the bridegroom appeared. He was short, and on one wrist were two white doves. He released them, and they flew everywhere in the room, flapping their wings in fright. The bridegroom was obliged to catch them, as each had a wedding ring attached to a leg, and my boredom vanished as I watched him scrambling over sideboards, tables and chairs.

After he had retrieved the doves the guests were ushered into a dining room, where several large tables were laden with desserts that looked delicious. Experience had taught me that the appearances are deceiving; by Western standards, at least, the Chinese are inferior dessert cooks. I needn't have worried, however, as no one offered us any.

We spread out, sitting wherever we pleased, and another silence descended on the group. When I saw that no one was touching any of the desserts it occurred to me that they might be waiting for the first move from me, the only foreigner present. So I reached for a cookie.

Everyone glared at me, and I realized I had committed a faux pas.

I didn't know what to do. I couldn't eat the cookie, and it would have been gauche to drop it back onto the table. So I held it. Interminably. First in my hand, then between my fingers, where it still melted, spilling crumbs over my dress. Occasionally someone still glowered at me as a reminder of my bad manners.

After another quarter hour of waiting, a servant came into the room carrying a porcelain bowl that contained a small statue of a goddess of the sea, Samudrah.

Then a man entered. His head was shaven, and he was dressed in Oriental robes. He was carrying a red silk cushion in one hand, a large knife in the other. He spoke in a patois that was a mixture of Chinese and Javanese, and seemed to be praying, At least the intonations of his voice indicated to me that he might be praying. The prayer was interminable, and again I was bored.

I asked the man sitting next to me if he could explain the significance of the knife. He said it was needed to kill any bad spirits that might be present. I couldn't resist joking, an unfortunate habit of mine when I'm bored or out of sorts, and suggested that the knife might be used to cut the umbilical cords of the couple's future children. He replied, in all seriousness, that bamboo was used to cut the cords. Now I understand why so many newborn babies in Indonesia die of tetanus.

After he had finished praying, the priest handed the knife to the bridegroom, who went to an adjoining bedroom, and in full view of the entire company, placed it beneath the pillows on the bed. Many Indonesian homes have no doors between rooms, as they would impede the flow of air, so everyone could see this symbolic act.

According to ancient custom the groom may kill the bride if she is not a virgin. This practice is no longer followed, but a girl who has had premarital sex may be sent back to her family in disgrace. Strangely, this same custom is observed halfway around the world in Saudi Arabia.

After the groom rejoined the guests, a long line of servants paraded through the room, each bearing a wedding gift that was shown to the guests. These included lipsticks and other cosmetics that were difficult to obtain in Indonesia in 1968, sandals, beautifully embroidered house slippers and lovely silk robes. At the end of the procession were two servants, each carrying a hand-carved white coffin. I was so startled I asked someone sitting near me about these "boxes." He not only confirmed that they were coffins, but was deeply impressed by this thoughtful gift. Ultimately the couple would need them, and meanwhile they would be stored somewhere in their house.

The ceremonies lasted five or six hours, and by the time they were finished I was ravenous. But no one touched a bite of the food spread out on the tables. I was told it would be eaten the following day by the bridal couple and their families. I hurried back to my hotel for a meal.

Some months later in Indonesia I was invited by some business associates to take part in a hunting expedition. Firearms don't frighten me, and I've hunted several times. But I was a bit frightened when I was told we were going to hunt leopards.

We flew to the island of Sumatra, where our caravan of jeeps plunged into a forest of huge trees with masses of twisted, gnarled branches. When possible we avoided driving directly under these branches, and I was told that poisonous snakes often drop down out of the trees onto their unwary victims. By the end of the day I had spent so much time staring up at the branches that the back of my neck ached.

That night we slept in tents, and bowls of water were placed at the entrances to keep out ants. They had no effect, and my tent was alive with ants, spiders and small snakes, which I was assured were nonpoisonous. I didn't close my eyes all night, and was exhausted when we set out again the following morning.

The jungle was so thick we had to cut our way through the undergrowth with machetes. There were beautiful birds everywhere, but they were strangely silent. They never sang and occasionally made eerie squawking sounds. We gathered some eggs and cooked them for lunch on a fire we made beside a small stream.

While we were eating, a large snake slid silently across my feet, and I screamed. My friends soothed me by saying that this particular kind of snake was harmless, provided one doesn't step on them, and I was wearing knee-high boots.

By our third day in the jungle we had seen no leopards, and I'd had enough. But my friends told me the fun was just about to begin. We had never intended to shoot leopards, they said. Instead we were hunting for Communists.

I was horrified by the prospect of killing human beings for sport, but they were serious. After the left-wing government of President Sukarno collapsed, many of his most rabid Communist supporters fled to the jungles and continued to hide out there.

My friends calmly said I shouldn't be shocked, that they had learned the "sport" from the Dutch in the 1920s and '30s, when Indonesia had still been a colony. I have no way of knowing whether they spoke the truth, and merely report what they told me.

I was adamant in my refusal to participate in the grisly expedition, and I insisted firmly that I be returned to civilization without delay. I had spoiled their fun and the hunt was abandoned.

A short time before I left Djakarta I was invited to the theater by a wealthy, cultivated Indonesian couple, and being a theater buff I eagerly accepted. They called for me in their limousine, and we drove interminably through badly lighted streets.

When we climbed out of the car we had to walk through mud littered with the remains of fruit being sold by the owners of small stands. I really shouldn't say we walked—we slid. Ultimately we came to an iron gate, which was opened for us and then locked behind us, and after another walk we came to a tent. Our seats were near the front, and I was able to look directly up at the sky through a large hole in the canvas.

The curtain rose on the first act, and we saw giants confronting traitors. The faces of the giants were painted white, and those of the traitors were painted red. An orchestra of instruments unlike any I had ever seen began to play dissonant musical chords. The actors kicked each other, synchronizing their movements with marvelous accuracy. This went on for a full hour.

The second act was more of the same, the only change being a different backdrop. The third act was a precise repetition of the first two. Through all this monotonous action a narrator spoke endlessly, and seemed never to pause for breath. After spending several months in Indonesia I had picked up some of the rudiments of the local language, but I couldn't understand one word the narrator said.

Finally I asked my hostess what he was saying.

"I don't know, either," she said. "He's speaking in an old Javanese dialect. But his voice is beautiful, don't you think?"

Politeness forced me to agree, but I couldn't help wondering why people attended the theater if they couldn't understand what was being said on the stage.

A sudden tropical rainstorm soaked us during the third act. But we had ample time to dry off.

When the giants appeared for the fourth act they sat down. This made sense to me, as they had been exercising incessantly for the better part of five hours. By now I was so bored I wanted to take a nap, and asked my hostess how much longer the performance would last. It was customary, she told me, for plays in Indonesia to run anywhere from nine to eleven hours. I steeled myself for the rest of the ordeal.

I was urged not to become impatient. Soon the Princess would appear on the stage, and then the play would become exciting.

Well, the Princess made her entrance, and proved to be an actress with the longest hair I had ever seen. She glided to the center of the stage and began to move her hands. Soon it occurred to me that she was repeating the same series of hand movements.

At last I turned to my hostess. "I don't know if I'm

counting correctly," I said, "but it seems to me the Princess is repeating every movement twelve times."

She sighed. "Isn't it a shame? Before this new era of modernization every movement was repeated seventeen to twenty-three times."

I could only be grateful I had come to a modern indonesia, but that was small comfort.

Soon after the fifth act began I heard several empty chairs being tipped over, and was stunned when I saw a huge boa constrictor gliding along the floor. I was so frightened I couldn't move.

My friend's husband tried to calm me. "They're harmless if you don't touch them or molest them. They aren't poisonous, you know. They just strangle their victims."

I watched the snake as it drew closer to me, refusing to allow myself to faint. It won't poison me, I thought, it'll just strangle me.

The snake decided I wasn't worth the bother, perhaps because it disliked the odor of the mosquito repellant I had smeared on my legs. It moved off, then coiled up under a seat and went to sleep.

I was still so terrified I kept watch on it until it awakened and moved away. Then it was my turn to sleep, and I dozed. Now, at least, I knew why the gates were locked. Indonesian audiences couldn't escape from the theater in panic.

At three-thirty in the morning I was awakened by the roar of exploding firecrackers. At last the performance had come to an end. It is obvious that I've never again accepted an invitation to the theater in Indonesia.

In 1961 I had an extraordinary experience when I was invited to the dedication of the new city of Brasilia, which was built as the capital of Brazil and would be utilized exclusively as the country's capital.

From the air its huge monuments and enormous buildings looked impressive. From the ground, however, I obtained a far different impression. The city was unfinished, no sidewalks had been built and thanks to several days of steady rain, I waded through mud that was often knee-high.

I found the inadequate workmanship astonishing. It was a common sight to see large nails protruding from doors and walls made of beautiful wood. The new hotels provided adventures of their own. I stayed in a handsome hotel that had just opened its doors—and I couldn't wait to leave. The bathroom faucets didn't work properly, so the floors were awash, and alive with armies of roaches swimming in formation.

I've been asked which of the countries I've visited has the worst automobile drivers, and friends have suggested that the prize be awarded to Belgium, Turkey or Iran. Not so. Argentina stands first by a wide margin.

While being driven by a chauffeur in Mar del Plata, a city on the Atlantic, we suffered three collisions with other cars in the course of one short ride. Nobody exchanged license numbers or insurance information. In fact, no one even bothered to stop.

My driver explained that it would be a waste of time to halt, and that too much work would be involved. "Anyway," he said, "if I hit somebody today, he'll hit me next week, and we can't spend the whole day filling papers with information."

There is a total disregard for pedestrians, and bus riding is an extraordinary experience. Bus drivers engage in a competition, on which they frequently make wagers, to be the first to reach the end of the run. So they drive on sidewalks when they think it will save time, they cut corners and they send pedestrians flying. If a driver condescends to stop for an insistent passenger who wants to disembark, he pauses for only a second or two, and takes off again very quickly, often slamming the door on some unfortunate passenger who finds his arm or leg is caught. When this happens the passenger is obliged to shout or scream, and the driver opens the door just enough to allow the poor wretch to pull free.

One of my most memorable trips was the visit to Saudi Arabia, Kuwait and other countries on the Persian Gulf, which I made in company with my husband in 1975. I had previously visited Lebanon and Iran, and having seen such modern cities as Beirut and Teheran, I was totally unprepared for such a drastically different way of life.

The tall buildings of Kuwait look modern from the air, so I was astonished when I moved out of our air-conditioned jet into a sauna bath. The airport thermometer registered over 130 degrees Fahrenheit, and the humidity was frightful. I was wearing a nylon shirt that became glued to my body, my skin became red and stayed that way until we left. Kuwait may be modern, but it has no sidewalks, no shops and no stores. Retail merchandise is sold only at a central bazaar, and to a Westerner the absence of shops depersonalizes a city. What surprised me most on the drive from the airport to our hotel was the complete lack of pedestrians anywhere. Kuwait resembled a ghost city, and with good reason: The combination of the heat and a threatened sandstorm blowing in from the desert kept people off the streets.

To me the most shocking sight in both Kuwait and Saudi Arabia is that of the native women. They wear veils and *yashmaks,* loose-fitting garments that cover them from the tops of their heads to their shoes, and only because they walk upright are they identifiable as human beings. No child could recognize its mother, no husband would know his wife in a veil and *yashmak.* The ugliness of these shrouds is beyond description, and is not accidental.

The old Islamic codes still prevail in these lands, and women are creatures apart, their rights strictly limited. According to Moslem tradition a woman is endowed with such a potent erotic nature that she will seduce any man who sees her. Therefore she stays hidden when she ventures beyond the confines of her own home, partly for her own protection and also for that of any male passerby.

In neither Kuwait nor Saudi Arabia did I meet even one local woman. The wives and daughters of the men with whom we did business stayed behind the grilled, locked gates of their *hareems,* precisely as their mothers and grandmothers have done for more than one thousand years. It does little good for a woman who believes in sexual equality to condemn the system. I was regarded as something of a freak by the men with whom we did business, and I'm sure my husband was considered insane for "allowing" me to appear unveiled and participate in the conferences.

I've been told that women from Kuwait and Saudi Arabia discard their *yashmaks* and veils the moment they travel beyond the borders of their own countries. I know, in fact, that many Arabian women of means wear French designer dresses under their shrouds!

I was told a story, on good authority, that illustrates the dilemma of people from these old-fashioned Arab countries. A young man and a young woman, both from leading Kuwait families, were sent to England, and attended schools there at the same time. They happened to meet, liked each other and began to date regularly. Frequently they had dinner together in London, they went to the theater and they danced at supper clubs. I have no idea whether they had an affair, but they were not chaperoned when they went together.

Since that time both have returned to Kuwait. The girl has seen the young man—from a distance—but doesn't dare speak to him. He, of course, doesn't even recognize her in her veil and *yashmak*. Only if he applies through his family to her family for her hand in marriage will they ever meet again, at least in Kuwait. I don't know if he wants to marry her. If not, their paths cannot cross again.

Only at our hotel, which was large, modern and comfortable, did I see Arab women in modern dress. Without exception they came from Egypt and other less backward Islamic nations. They could appear at the swimming pool in bikinis, but the moment they left the hotel they, too, wore all-encompassing robes and veils.

I swam in the hotel pool just once. The heat was stultifying, the water was hot and I was horrified when guests standing at the side used the pool as a toilet. I complained to the lifeguard, who thought I was making a fuss about nothing. Almost needless to say, I threw away my bathing suit and scrubbed myself with alcohol in the bath.

In Kuwait I saw large numbers of lovely homes built by the government for nomads who came in from the desert to visit the city. These houses seldom were occupied, the nomads preferring to pitch their tents and tether their camels on the extensive lawns.

Only now are the first factories being built in Kuwait. Virtually everything from steel, glass and concrete used in the construction of buildings to consumer goods is imported. Citizens of stature know they are behind the times, and currently there is a rush to put up badly needed fertilizer plants, but the basic situation there is not healthy because oil reserves will be exhausted in about thirty years. So, for the present, they are stashing away as much as their oil can earn.

Dhahran and Bahrein on the Persian Gulf were similar to Kuwait. The men with whom we did business were friendly, even though somewhat uncomfortable in my presence. I saw a few veiled women from a distance.

The old Moslem laws are more strictly observed in Saudi Arabia than in any of the other places we visited. At noon men pour into the streets by the tens of thousands from their offices and factories, making the cities look like playgrounds, but no women mingle with them. I caught glimpses of a few women, heavily veiled, in the bazaars, but never encountered them anywhere else.

The Saudis take the teachings of the Koran literally. When they visit the West they may drive Rolls Royces, go to nightclubs with blondes and wear three-thousand-dollar wristwatches, but at home their lifestyle is very simple. They dress in Arab robes and wear no jewelry; they live in simply furnished houses that are bare of paintings and other wall decorations, and they drive small, cheap cars. I'm told they give expensive gifts to their wives and daughters, but the ladies can show off their diamonds, gold and French gowns only to each other within the confines of their own *hareems*.

Peter and I were entertained by a number of prominent Saudi businessmen, eating dinner at their homes because there are no restaurants in the country. Our hosts carefully washed their hands before each meal, and we were expected to do the same. With good reason. They use no utensils when they eat, and either they served us our portions with their bare hands or all of us dipped into a common pot.

To my intense disappointment I didn't meet one woman in Saudi Arabia. I suspect that wives and daughters were kept secluded because my husband was an outsider. On several occasions I hinted, rather delicately, that I would have loved to meet the ladies of the house and see their living quarters, but my oblique comments were ignored. Perhaps our hosts thought I was too forward, and didn't want their women to catch my dangerous freedom virus. Now that I think of it, not only were wives and daughters invisible, but I saw no women servants in the country, either.

In spite of their restricted society the Saudis are urbane, cosmopolitan men, many of them having traveled extensively in the United States, Great Britain and Europe. They are warm hosts and honorable in their business dealings. Like all good Moslems they neither drink nor serve alcoholic beverages, although I'm told they're no strangers to whiskey when they visit the West.

Their offices are open, and not only can the president of the company be seen at his labors by the lowest clerk and office boy, but he can also see them. I found it strange that only members of the aristocracy work, and they work hard. Clerical and menial positions are held by Egyptians, Pakistanis, and Palestinians.

To say the least, the atmosphere is informal. Everyone is on familiar terms with the top executives. One day, when we were engaged in a meeting with the president of a large company and several of his close associates, we were interrupted by a toothless old man in a ragged robe who wandered into the room. We were discussing a deal involving large sums of money, but no one minded in the least when the old man interrupted to extract the equivalent of five dollars from the president for a laundry bill.

We were told a story that, I think, amply illustrates the Saudi character. The country is an absolute monarchy, and the crown has the powers of life and death over all of the country's people. Well, a servant in the employ of the king owned a small plot of land adjacent to an extensive property that belonged to the king. Inadvertantly the king encroached on the man's land.

The servant went to court, and the judge—necessarily a member of the royal family—ordered the king to restore the property. The servant is still in the employ of the crown, and no attempt has been made to punish him for his temerity.

Of all the countries I've visited I found Taiwan the most fascinating. Their mountains are beautiful, but

I've seen lovely scenery in many places. What interested me was the sensitivity of the people and the strange combination of brusque manners and excessive politeness.

I spent some time living in the home of a wealthy Chinese woman, and was dumbfounded by her daily routine. Each morning she arose early and plucked her hairline, the Chinese believing that a high forehead is a sign of intelligence. Then she devoted several hours to a manicure, pedicure and massages with perfumed oils. By afternoon, if nothing interfered with her schedule, she would go to a pagoda, light several tall, thin candles and after writing her secret wishes on slips of paper, offer these to the gods. These wishes seldom came true, but that didn't stop her from going regularly to the pagoda.

One day in Taipei, the capital, while I was holding a meeting with a local businessman, I invited him to dinner that evening and included his wife. He nodded his acceptance, his face creased in the permanent smile to which Western travelers in the Orient soon become accustomed.

I arrived a few minutes early at the restaurant, and on the dot of 8:00 P.M. the businessman and his wife arrived, accompanied by twenty-two sons, daughters, in-laws and grandchildren. I learned that my invitation, according to Chinese custom, automatically included the entire family, and the manager of the restaurant had to give us a private room to accommodate my party!

One habit to which I can't acclimate, anywhere in the Far East, is the total lack of table manners in the Chinese. Breeding is irrelevant; in all classes, such manners are unknown. The object of eating is to propel one's food from bowl or plate to mouth, and how one achieves this feat is the individual's private business. Seeing a Chinese eat noodles is a sight I'd rather be spared, and I've learned, when in the Orient, to look away when a table companion eats fish and spits bones into his bowl.

The Chinese rarely invite visitors into their homes, but I wanted to see a typical businessman's house, and after hinting broadly on a number of occasions I finally received an invitation.

My hostess and I exchanged endless bows before we sat down in her lacquered living room, and then she served an endless variety of dishes. At last came the triumph of the day, the family's pet dog, which had been killed and cooked in my honor. I wasn't feigning when I pleaded a sudden illness!

Somewhat later, in Hong Kong, I did business with a Chinese who frequently invited me to dinner. He took me to the best restaurants, but I was always somewhat uncomfortable in his presence because he rarely conversed. I could not accustom myself to his long silences.

After I went from Hong Kong to Indonesia he visited me in Djakarta. I did literally nothing to encourage him, but he was persistent in his pursuit of the friendship, and finally it occurred to me that he had a personal interest in me. I didn't reciprocate, but he continued to visit me.

One day, out of the blue, he informed me that I had beautiful hair. It was the first personal remark he had ever addressed to me, and I felt slightly embarrassed, so I laughed. He seemed offended, and I couldn't understand what I had done to hurt his feelings.

I mentioned the incident to a Chinese friend, who

told me the man from Hong Kong had proposed marriage to me.

The idea was so farfetched that I refused to believe her, feeling certain she was teasing me. She claimed she meant it, but I knew better.

Then I married Peter, and a short time later I received a nasty, indignant letter from the gentleman in Hong Kong. He declared that I had jilted him and had no right to marry someone else when I was engaged to him.

I've checked with other friends who know the Orient, and they tell me the Hong Kong businessman had been encouraged by my acceptance of his dinner invitations. If I had frowned or remained stone-faced when he had made his personal remark about my hair, he would have known I had rejected him. Instead I had laughed, which he had taken as an acceptance of his suit, and what I had interpreted as hurt on his part had been stunned pleasure.

Oh, well. Live and learn.

I'm still learning, which is the fun and in many ways the whole point of living.

My sons are young men, beginning to lead their own lives, and they give me great contentment.

I'm still making progress in my career, and I intend to remain active in the theater, too, and before long I'll be producing another play.

Only one goal is still unfulfilled. I want to establish a number of university scholarships for deserving young women. What I've done the hard way can be accomplished by others with less grinding work, less turmoil, and these scholarships will serve a double purpose. They will be an expression of my gratitude for being a woman. And they will be an expression of thanks to America for the freedom I've enjoyed here and the opportunities I've been given to create a substantial, useful life for myself in my adopted country.